EQUILIBRIUM

LEVEL YOUR LIFE

SUNIL KUMAR KODICHATH BE., MBA., Ph.D.

You will gain a new worldview.

Chennai • Bangalore

CLEVER FOX PUBLISHING
Chennai, India

Published by CLEVER FOX PUBLISHING 2023
Copyright © SUNIL KUMAR KODICHATH BE., MBA., Ph.D. 2023

All Rights Reserved.
ISBN: 978-93-56483-84-2

ACKNOWLEDGMENT

*T*his book is dedicated to my loved ones and the almighty and to my well-wishers who are having similar thoughts.

CONTENTS

INTRODUCTION

$\mathcal{P}$hilosophy is a vast and complex system of thought that encompasses a wide range of topics, from metaphysics and ethics to social justice and environmental stewardship. At the heart of Hindu philosophy are two key concepts: *karma* and *dharma*. *Karma* refers to the law of cause and effect, which holds that our actions have consequences, both in this life and in future lives. *Dharma*, on the other hand, refers to our duty or purpose in life and is closely tied to our spiritual development and ultimate liberation.

In this book, we will explore these concepts in depth, examining how they are interrelated and can guide us on the path of spiritual growth and self-realization. We will also explore a range of related topics, from the power of forgiveness to the relationship between *karma* and social justice, offering practical views and insights along the way.

As contrary to the statement "Ignorance is bliss", to experience bliss one needs to remove ignorance.

Each chapter in this book is designed to deepen our understanding of these key concepts and their practical applications in our lives. Whether we are seeking greater spiritual awareness and connection, or simply looking for ways to live more purposefully and joyfully, the principles of *karma* and *dharma* can serve as powerful guides on our journey. So, join us on this exploration of this philosophy and the path of *karma* and *dharma*, and discover the wisdom and insight that can transform your life.

Since these are very complex, inter-linked thoughts, it is advised that the readers make inline reading notes about the concepts and capture their respective points of view against each and then further deliberate and contemplate on all the complete notes towards the end to arrive at their way of life-principles.

Karma - Cause & Effect

CHAPTER 1

UNDERSTANDING KARMA AND DHARMA

*T*hese concepts offer a unique perspective on questions of morality, meaning, and purpose, and have shaped the spiritual and intellectual landscape of India and beyond. We will also explore how these concepts can be applied in practical ways, offering insights and tools for personal growth and ethical decision-making.

Karma is one of the most important concepts in Hindu philosophy, representing the idea that every action has a consequence that affects an individual's spiritual journey. The concept of karma is deeply tied to the belief in reincarnation, which holds that the accumulation of karma in one's current lifetime will determine their reincarnation in the next lifetime.

According to Hinduism, there are three types of *karma*: *sanchita karma*, *prarabdha karma* and, *kriyamana karma*. *Sanchita karma* refers to the accumulated *karma* from past lives. It is the total of all the *karma* that has been accumulated throughout an individual's previous lives. *Prarabdha karma* refers to the current *karma* that is being experienced in this lifetime. It is the *karma* that has been chosen for the current lifetime, and it cannot be changed. *Kriyamana karma*, on the other hand, refers to the *karma* that is being created in the present moment. This type of *karma* is under an individual's control, and it can be changed by making conscious choices.

Understanding the different types of *karma* is essential in understanding how our actions shape our spiritual journey and what we can do to make positive changes. While *sanchita karma* is not directly under an individual's control, understanding it can help individuals identify patterns in their lives and make positive changes in their current actions. *Prarabdha karma*, meanwhile, serves as a reminder that actions have consequences and that individuals must take responsibility for their actions. *Kriyamana karma* is the type of *karma* that is most under an individual's control, as it is created in the present moment. <u>By making conscious choices, individuals can create positive kriyamana karma and work towards creating a better future for themselves and others.</u>

In Hinduism, reincarnation is a fundamental concept that underpins the idea of *karma*. Reincarnation is the belief that the soul is eternal and is reborn into a new body after death. This cycle of birth and rebirth is known as *samsara*. The soul takes on a new body in each lifetime, and the circumstances of that life are determined by the accumulated *karma* from previous lifetimes.

The concept of reincarnation is closely linked to the idea of *karma*, as *karma* is the measure of an individual's actions and their consequences. *Karma* can be both positive and negative, and the accumulation of positive *karma* leads to a better future life, while negative *karma* leads to a more challenging future life.

Therefore, the way we act in our current life will determine the nature of our next life. If we live a virtuous life, following the principles of *dharma* and acting with kindness and compassion towards others, we will accumulate positive *karma* and be reborn into a better life in the future. On the other hand, if we act selfishly and cruelly, harming others, we will accumulate negative *karma* and be reborn into a more challenging life.

Understanding the relationship between *karma* and reincarnation can help us make choices that positively impact our future lives. By living a life of *dharma* and compassion, we can accumulate positive *karma* and ensure a better future for ourselves and those around us.

<u>Dharma is a fundamental concept in Hindu philosophy that refers to an individual's duty or moral obligation in life.</u> It encompasses the values, principles, and responsibilities that guide an individual's actions and decisions. The concept of *dharma* is closely connected to the idea of *karma*, where one's actions have consequences that shape their spiritual journey.

Living in accordance with *dharma* means fulfilling one's responsibilities and duties with integrity, honesty, and compassion. It involves making choices that align with one's values and principles and that benefit the individual and society as a whole. Following *dharma* can lead to positive karmic consequences, as individuals who live in accordance with their *dharma* are believed to be fulfilling their spiritual purpose.

In Hindu philosophy, the concept of *karma* is not limited to the individual. It can also extend to groups or societies as a whole. Collective *karma* is the idea that the actions of a group or society can have a karmic impact, which means that the positive or negative actions of individuals within a society can affect the overall karmic balance of the group. This idea emphasizes the interconnectedness of all beings and highlights the importance of individual actions in shaping the world around us.

Collective *karma* can manifest in various forms, such as natural disasters, social unrest, or economic downturns. The collective actions of society can either create positive or negative *karma*, and it is essential to understand the consequences of these actions. For example, if a society values compassion, honesty, and integrity, the collective *karma* of that society will reflect those values. Conversely, if a society promotes violence, greed, and corruption, the collective *karma* of that society will reflect those values.

Understanding the concept of collective *karma* can help individuals recognize the impact of their actions on their community and inspire them to take responsibility for their role in shaping society. By working towards creating positive collective *karma*, individuals can contribute to a better world for themselves and others. The concept of collective *karma* reminds us that our actions have consequences, and we must be mindful of the impact we have on the world around us.

In Hindu philosophy, intention is considered to be a key component of *karma*. The quality of an action is determined not just by the action itself, but also by the intention behind it. If the intention behind an action is positive, then the karmic consequence will also be positive even if the outcome of the action itself may not be favorable.

This is why mindfulness is often emphasized as a means of becoming more aware of one's intentions and actions. By cultivating a greater sense of self-awareness, individuals can start noticing the intentions behind their actions and make more conscious choices. This can lead to a shift towards more positive intentions and actions, which can in turn lead to positive karmic consequences.

Practicing mindfulness can involve a range of techniques, from meditation to self-reflection. The goal is to become more present in the moment and more aware of one's thoughts and feelings. By doing so, individuals can notice patterns in their behavior and recognize the intentions that underlie their actions.

Mindfulness can be especially useful in situations where emotions are running high or there is a tendency to act impulsively. By taking a moment to pause and reflect on one's intentions, individuals can avoid actions that may have negative karmic consequences. This can also lead to a more positive spiritual journey and a greater sense of fulfillment and well-being.

The relationship between free will and determinism in the concept of *karma* is complex and has been debated by philosophers for centuries. On one hand, *karma* suggests that our actions and their consequences are predetermined by our past actions and accumulated *karma*. This implies a certain degree of determinism in shaping one's life. On the other hand, the concept of *karma* also suggests that individuals have the ability to make choices in the present moment that can shape their future.

<u>While past actions may create certain conditions and predispositions, it is ultimately up to the individual to make choices that either reinforce or mitigate the effects of past karma.</u> For example, if an individual has accumulated negative *karma* through harmful actions in the past, they can still choose to engage in positive actions in the present to mitigate the negative effects of their past *karma*.

Furthermore, the concept of *karma* also suggests that the intention behind one's actions is equally important as the action itself. This means that even if one is predisposed to certain outcomes due to past *karma*, the intention behind their actions can still shape its karmic consequences.

In essence, the concept of *karma* suggests that while certain conditions and predispositions may shape one's life, individuals still have the ability to make choices and exercise free will in the present moment that can shape their future.

The connection between *dharma* and *karma*, and how living in accordance with *dharma* can lead to positive karmic consequences:

One's *dharma* is believed to influence the accumulation of *karma*, which, in turn, shapes one's spiritual journey and determines their reincarnation in the next life. Therefore, living in accordance with *dharma* is crucial for those seeking spiritual growth and a positive karmic outcome.

The concept of *dharma* can also extend beyond an individual's personal responsibilities and encompass broader social and cultural obligations. In this sense, *dharma* can provide the framework for creating a just and ethical society. By fulfilling their *dharma*, individuals can contribute to the betterment of society, leading to positive karmic consequences for themselves and others.

Adrishta is a concept in Hindu philosophy that refers to the unseen force that affects the consequences of an action. It is often described as the link between an action and its result. While some actions may have immediate and obvious consequences, others may not show their effects until much later. This is where the concept of *adrishta* comes into play. It is believed that this unseen force can cause karmic consequences to manifest later in life, even if the original action was committed long ago.

Adrishta is sometimes compared to the concept of the boomerang effect or the law of cause and effect. Just as throwing a boomerang can cause it to return to the thrower, actions can create unseen forces that return to the doer, impacting their present and future lives. This is why it is important to be mindful of one's actions and to consider the potential consequences of those actions, even if they may not be immediately apparent.

Understanding the role of *adrishta* can also help individuals to let go of attachment to the outcome of their actions. *Adrishta* is also related to grace or blessing to convey that any outcome is a combination of man's effort and the almighty's enablement. Just because a particular action does not immediately lead to the desired result does not mean that it was not worthwhile or that it will not have an impact in the future. By trusting in the power of *adrishta* and the law of cause and effect, individuals can focus on doing what is right and virtuous, rather than being driven solely by the desire for a particular outcome.

The relationship between the concept of *karma* and the law of cause and effect in modern physics can be traced back to the interconnectedness of all things. In physics, the law of cause and effect suggests that every action has a reaction and that these reactions can have consequences that reverberate throughout the entire universe. Similarly, the concept of *karma* suggests that every action has a consequence and that these consequences can have an impact on the individual's spiritual journey.

<u>Both the concepts of karma and dharma suggest that there is a deep interconnectedness between all things in the universe.</u> Every action, whether in physics or the spiritual realm, has consequences that extend beyond the immediate moment. In physics, these consequences can manifest as physical phenomena or changes in the state of matter. In the spiritual realm, these consequences can manifest as positive or negative karmic consequences that impact an individual's future lives.

By exploring the relationship between these two concepts, individuals can gain a deeper understanding of the nature of reality and the interconnectedness of all things. This understanding can inspire individuals to be more mindful of their actions and the consequences they may have, both in the physical world and in their spiritual journey. Ultimately, the connection between *karma* and the law of cause and effect in modern physics highlights the importance of taking responsibility for our actions and the impact they may have on the world around us.

The concept of *karma* suggests that every action has a consequence, and those consequences can be positive or negative, depending on the nature of the action. This means that every individual has a responsibility to act in a way that aligns with their values and beliefs to accumulate positive *karma*. Understanding the karmic consequences of one's actions can provide a powerful motivation for individuals to behave in an ethical and moral manner.

Similarly, the concept of *dharma* provides a framework for ethical decision-making. *Dharma* is the moral law that governs the universe and the duty that each individual has to fulfill their role in the world. Living in accordance with *dharma* means acting in a way that is in alignment with one's duties and responsibilities, and upholding the moral principles that guide society. This can include things like treating others with kindness and respect, contributing to the well-being of one's community, and being honest and truthful in one's dealings.

By understanding the concepts of *karma* and *dharma*, individuals can gain a deeper understanding of their ethical responsibilities and make more informed decisions about how to act in the world. This can help to promote a more just and equitable society, where individuals are motivated to act in the best interests of themselves and others, and where ethical principles are upheld and respected.

Self-reflection and self-awareness are two key components of living a life in accordance with *dharma* and understanding one's karmic journey. By taking the time to reflect on past actions and choices, individuals can gain insight into their motivations and intentions. This self-awareness allows for a deeper understanding of how one's actions may impact their spiritual journey and the world around them.

Self-reflection can be a difficult process, as it requires an honest and sometimes uncomfortable examination of one's actions and beliefs. However, it is an essential part of personal growth and spiritual development. Through self-reflection, individuals can identify patterns of behavior or thought that may be negatively impacting their karmic journey, to make conscious choices to change them.

Self-awareness is also important in understanding the intentions behind one's actions. In Hindu philosophy, the intention behind an action is just as important as the action itself. By becoming more aware of one's intentions, individuals can ensure that their actions are aligned with *dharma* and will lead to positive karmic consequences.

Overall, self-reflection and self-awareness are integral parts of understanding one's karmic journey and living a life in accordance with *dharma*. By taking the time to reflect and become more self-aware, individuals can make conscious choices that positively impact their spiritual journey and the world around them.

CHAPTER 2

OPPORTUNITIES AND CONSEQUENCES

One of the most common dilemmas that we face in our daily lives is whether to take advantage of an opportunity that presents itself, even if it means potentially disadvantaging someone else. In the Hindu tradition, this question is intimately tied to the concept of *karma*, which suggests that all actions have consequences, both for us and for others. In this chapter, we will explore the complex ethical dimensions of opportunity and ambition, considering how the principles of *karma* and *dharma* can help us navigate these challenges with compassion and wisdom. We will also examine the relationship between individual desire and collective responsibility, asking how we can cultivate a sense of purpose and meaning that aligns with our highest values.

The concept of opportunities is essential in understanding how individuals can shape their lives and achieve their goals. An opportunity can be defined as a chance or opening that allows an individual to achieve something they desire or to take advantage of a situation that may not always be available. Opportunities can present themselves in various forms, such as a new job offer, a chance to travel, or even a simple invitation to a social event. Understanding the nature of opportunities and how they arise is crucial in recognizing and making the most of them.

Opportunities can arise in unexpected ways and at unexpected times. Sometimes opportunities can arise through personal connections or chance encounters, and at other times they can be the result of hard work and dedication. <u>Recognizing opportunities requires mindfulness and an openness to possibilities.</u> It involves being aware of one's surroundings and paying attention to the people and situations that present themselves.

Making the most of opportunities requires taking action and seizing the moment. It involves taking risks and stepping outside one's comfort zone. When individuals take advantage of opportunities, they can experience positive consequences such as personal growth, new experiences, and success. However, failing to take advantage of opportunities can also have consequences, such as missed potential and regret.

Understanding the nature of opportunities also involves recognizing the impact of privilege and access to opportunities on an individual's life journey. It requires acknowledging how systemic inequalities can limit opportunities for certain individuals and working towards creating a more equitable society.

Understanding the nature of opportunities and how they arise involves being mindful, recognizing the various forms opportunities can take, and being willing to take action to make the most of them. It also involves recognizing the impact of privilege and systemic inequalities on access to opportunities and working towards creating a more just and equitable society.

In ancient Greek philosophy, the concept of *kairos* was regarded as the opportune moment for action. Unlike *chronos*, which refers to chronological time, *kairos* is subjective and dependent on context. It refers to a critical moment, a turning point, or a window of opportunity where one can take action that can lead to a favorable outcome. <u>Kairos is a moment that is not to be missed, as it may not come again.</u>

Recognizing and seizing the moment is an essential aspect of success in life. One must develop the skill of distinguishing *kairos* moments from everyday events. It requires an understanding of the context and the ability to read the signs, whether they are external or internal. Timing is crucial when it comes to seizing opportunities, and one must learn to be patient and attentive, waiting for the right moment to act.

However, failure to recognize and act upon a *kairos* moment can result in missed opportunities, regret, and missed potential. These moments can sometimes be fleeting, and once they are gone, they may never come again. It is important to be aware of one's goals, values, and aspirations and to be alert for opportunities that align with them.

The concept of *kairos* is an essential aspect of ancient Greek philosophy that emphasizes the importance of recognizing and seizing the opportune moment for action. It encourages individuals to be mindful, patient, and attentive in their lives and to be aware of the potential opportunities that may arise. By developing the skill of recognizing *kairos* moments, individuals can take advantage of opportunities that can lead to positive outcomes and avoid the regret of missed opportunities.

Mindfulness is the practice of being fully present and aware of one's thoughts, feelings, and surroundings. It can be a powerful tool for recognizing and seizing opportunities in life. By practicing mindfulness, individuals can cultivate a heightened awareness of the present moment, which can help them recognize opportunities that might otherwise go unnoticed.

When individuals are more present and aware, they are also more attuned to their own needs and desires. This can help them recognize opportunities that align with their values and goals. For example, if someone is looking for a new job, practicing mindfulness can help them be more aware of job openings and networking opportunities that might arise.

Moreover, mindfulness can help individuals remain calm and focused in the face of challenges, which can enable them to recognize and capitalize on unexpected opportunities. For instance, if someone experiences a setback in their career, practicing mindfulness can help them stay centered and open to new possibilities that might emerge.

In addition, mindfulness can help individuals stay grounded in the present moment, which can prevent them from getting lost in worries or regrets about the past, or anxieties about the future. This can allow them to fully engage with the opportunities that are available to them right now.

Overall, mindfulness can be a powerful tool for recognizing and seizing opportunities in life. By cultivating a heightened awareness of the present moment, individuals can be more attuned to their own needs and desires, remain calm and focused in the face of challenges, and stay grounded in the present moment.

The consequences of taking advantage of opportunities versus letting them pass by can have a significant impact on an individual's life journey. Seizing opportunities can lead to personal and professional growth, new experiences, and a sense of fulfillment. On the other hand, failing to take advantage of opportunities can lead to missed potential, regret, and a sense of stagnation.

When an opportunity arises, individuals must weigh the potential risks and benefits of taking action. While there may be a degree of uncertainty and risk involved in seizing an opportunity, there is also the potential for significant rewards. By contrast, letting opportunities pass by can lead to a sense of missed potential and regret. Individuals who let opportunities pass may find themselves wondering "what if?" or wishing they had taken a chance.

However, it is important to note that not all opportunities are created equal and individuals must be discerning in their decision-making. Some opportunities may be distractions or not aligned with one's values or goals. In such cases, letting them pass by may actually be the wisest decision.

Ultimately, the consequences of taking advantage of opportunities versus letting them pass by depend on an individual's unique circumstances, goals, and values. However, it is important to approach opportunities with a sense of mindfulness and discernment, weighing the potential risks and benefits before making a decision. By doing so, individuals can make informed decisions that lead to positive outcomes and growth while avoiding missed potential and regret.

The impact of privilege and access to opportunities on an individual's life journey is a complex and nuanced topic. Individuals who have access to opportunities and privileges are often able to achieve more success and reach their goals more easily than those who do not. However, it's important to recognize that not all individuals have the same level of access to opportunities due to societal and systemic factors such as race, gender, socioeconomic status, and geographic location.

These factors can create significant barriers that limit an individual's ability to access education, job opportunities, and other resources that can help them achieve their goals. For example, individuals from low-income families may have limited access to quality education, which can limit their ability to pursue certain careers or advance in their fields.

Moreover, privilege and access to opportunities can shape an individual's path in life by providing them with more resources and support. For example, individuals who come from affluent families may have access to better healthcare, better education, and more networking opportunities, which can help them achieve their goals more easily than those who do not have these resources.

However, it's important to recognize that privilege and access to opportunities can also have negative consequences. Individuals who have access to more opportunities and resources may become complacent and less driven to achieve their goals. Additionally, privilege and access to opportunities can lead to a sense of entitlement and a lack of empathy for those who do not have the same access to resources.

<u>Overall, it's important to recognize the impact of privilege and access to opportunities on an individual's life journey and work towards creating a more equitable society where everyone has equal access to resources and opportunities.</u>

In our pursuit of success, we often focus on seizing opportunities that come our way without considering their ethical implications. However, every opportunity comes with a set of consequences, and our actions can have an impact on others. This topic explores the ethical implications of taking advantage of opportunities and the impact that one's actions can have on others.

When presented with an opportunity, it is essential to consider the consequences of our actions, particularly on others. For example, taking advantage of a job opportunity in a developing country at the expense of local workers could have negative consequences for the community. On the other hand, using our privilege and resources to create opportunities for others can have a positive impact on society.

Making ethical choices when presented with opportunities requires a deep understanding of the potential consequences of our actions. We must consider the impact on society, the environment, and the economy. By considering the long-term consequences of our actions, we can make choices that contribute to positive outcomes for all.

In addition, it is important to recognize that our actions can impact others, and we have a responsibility to ensure that our choices do not harm those around us. This means taking into account the impact on marginalized groups and ensuring that we do not exploit their vulnerabilities.

The ethical implications of taking advantage of opportunities are significant, and it is our responsibility to ensure that we make choices that contribute to positive outcomes for all. By considering the consequences of our actions and recognizing our impact on others, we can create a better world for everyone.

In our fast-paced world, distractions can often get in the way of recognizing and seizing opportunities. It is crucial for individuals to understand the difference between opportunities and distractions to make the most of their life journey. Distractions can take many forms, including social media, excessive television, and other forms of entertainment that consume an individual's time and attention.

Opportunities, on the other hand, can take many forms as well, and it is important for individuals to differentiate between genuine opportunities and distractions disguised as opportunities. Genuine opportunities often present themselves as challenges or risks that require individuals to step outside of their comfort zone. Distractions, on the other hand, often present themselves as easy or familiar paths that may not lead to growth or success.

To differentiate between opportunities and distractions, individuals can consider their personal values and goals. If an opportunity aligns with their values and helps them achieve their goals, it is likely to be a genuine opportunity. If an opportunity does not align with their values or distracts them from their goals, it may be a distraction.

It is also important for individuals to practice mindfulness to recognize opportunities and differentiate them from distractions. By being present in the moment and aware of their surroundings, individuals can more easily identify potential opportunities and take action.

In summary, understanding the difference between opportunities and distractions is crucial for individuals seeking to make the most of their life journey. By differentiating between the two and practicing mindfulness, individuals can recognize and seize genuine opportunities while avoiding distractions that may hinder their growth and success.

Missed opportunities can have a significant impact on an individual's life journey. When an opportunity arises, it often presents a chance for growth, learning, and development. However, when an individual misses an opportunity, it can lead to regret and missed potential. Regret is the feeling of disappointment that comes from not achieving a desired outcome, and it can have a negative impact on one's mental health and well-being. Missed potential refers to the opportunities that an individual could have pursued but didn't, resulting in unrealized growth and development.

It's important to reflect on missed opportunities and learn from them. When individuals miss opportunities, they can take the time to understand why they missed them and what they could have done differently. By understanding the root cause of the missed opportunity, individuals can make changes to their mindset or behavior to ensure they don't miss similar opportunities in the future.

Missed opportunities can also offer valuable lessons. They can help individuals understand what they truly want and what they value in life. These lessons can help individuals make more informed decisions and create a path for future opportunities.

It's also important to remember that missed opportunities are a natural part of life. No one can seize every opportunity that comes their way, and it's okay to miss some opportunities. It's important to focus on the opportunities that are truly important and align with one's values and goals.

Missed opportunities can lead to regret and missed potential, but they can also offer valuable lessons. Individuals can reflect on missed opportunities, learn from them, and use those lessons to create a path for future opportunities.

<u>Intuition and gut feelings can be powerful tools for recognizing and seizing opportunities.</u> While often difficult to define or quantify, intuition is a sense or feeling that one has about a situation or decision, often based on past experiences and knowledge. Gut feelings, on the other hand, are physical sensations in the body that are often associated with intuition.

<u>The development of intuition and trusting one's gut feelings can be a skill that is honed over time through self-reflection, meditation, and mindfulness practices.</u> By becoming more aware of their thoughts and emotions, individuals can learn to recognize when their intuition is guiding them toward an opportunity.

It is important to note that intuition and gut feelings should not be relied on alone when making decisions. Rather, they should be considered alongside rational analysis and other factors, such as one's values and priorities. Additionally, it is important to distinguish between intuition and irrational fears or biases that may be influencing one's thoughts and feelings.

Trusting one's intuition can be particularly important in situations where there is limited information or time to make a decision. By being attuned to their intuition, individuals may be able to recognize and act on opportunities that others overlook or dismiss.

Cultivating intuition and trusting gut feelings can also help individuals make choices that align with their values and goals, leading to greater fulfillment and purpose in life. It can also lead to greater self-awareness and confidence in decision-making, as individuals learn to trust their instincts and judgment.

Overall, recognizing the role of intuition and gut feelings in recognizing opportunities can be a valuable tool in making the most of one's life journey.

<u>Gratitude and humility are essential in recognizing and making the most of opportunities.</u> Gratitude involves acknowledging and appreciating the opportunities that come our way, while humility entails recognizing that these opportunities are not solely the result of our efforts, but rather a combination of factors, including luck, privilege, and the efforts of others. By cultivating these qualities, individuals can approach opportunities with a sense of humility, gratitude, and a desire to use them in a positive and ethical manner.

Practicing gratitude helps individuals shift their focus from what they lack to what they have, leading to a more positive and appreciative outlook on life. By being grateful for opportunities that come our way, we are better able to recognize and make the most of them. Gratitude also helps individuals remain humble and avoid becoming entitled or overly attached to a particular opportunity.

Humility is also crucial in recognizing and making the most of opportunities. It involves recognizing that opportunities are not solely the result of our efforts, but also a combination of factors such as luck, privilege, and the efforts of others. By acknowledging these factors, individuals can approach opportunities with a sense of perspective and a desire to use them in a positive and ethical manner.

In addition, cultivating gratitude and humility can also lead to greater generosity and empathy towards others. This can help individuals to recognize opportunities that may benefit not just themselves but also their communities and society as a whole.

Overall, the importance of gratitude and humility cannot be overstated when it comes to recognizing and making the most of opportunities. By cultivating these qualities, individuals can approach opportunities with a sense of perspective, gratitude, and a desire to use them in a positive and ethical manner that benefits not just themselves but also others.

CHAPTER 3

DESIRE, ATTACHMENT, AND KARMA

*D*esire is a fundamental aspect of the human experience, driving our motivations, aspirations, and dreams. In the Hindu tradition, desire is intimately connected to the concept of *karma*, which suggests that our actions are shaped by our intentions and that these intentions are in turn shaped by our desires. At the same time, the concept of *dharma* suggests that there is a duty or responsibility that accompanies every action and that this duty must be balanced against our desires and aspirations. In this chapter, we will explore the complex interplay between desire and duty in Hindu philosophy, examining how these concepts can help us understand the nature of motivation, ambition, and fulfillment. We will also explore how the practice of *karma* and *dharma* can help us cultivate a sense of balance and equanimity, even in the face of intense desire and temptation.

Desire is an intrinsic part of the human experience. We all have desires, ranging from basic needs like food and shelter to more complex desires such as love, success, and fame. Desire is a natural driving force that motivates us to take action and pursue our goals. However, desires can also be a source of suffering and negative *karma*.

The relationship between desire and *karma* is complex. According to Hindu and Buddhist philosophies, our desires and actions create karmic imprints that shape our future experiences. <u>Positive desires and actions lead to positive karmic consequences, while negative desires and actions lead to negative karmic consequences.</u> For example, if one desires and works towards helping others, they will create positive *karma*. But if one desires and works towards harming others, they will create negative *karma*.

Furthermore, desire can also lead to attachment, which can also have a significant impact on our karmic journey. Attachment is the feeling of dependence on or strong affection for someone or something. It can create a sense of possessiveness and obsession that can cause suffering when we are separated from the object of our attachment.

Therefore, understanding the nature of desire and its relationship to *karma* is essential to achieving spiritual growth and liberation. It involves recognizing the positive and negative aspects of our desires and actions and making conscious choices that align with our values and lead to positive karmic consequences. This requires cultivating mindfulness, non-attachment, and detachment from our desires and taking actions that benefit ourselves and others without causing harm. By doing so, we can achieve inner peace, happiness, and a positive karmic journey.

Attachment refers to the emotional bond we form with people, things, or ideas. It arises from a sense of identification and a feeling of ownership over something or someone. Attachment can shape our desires and actions in profound ways, leading us to pursue certain things or people and avoid others. It can influence our decisions, reactions, and overall outlook on life.

However, attachment can also lead to negative *karma*. When we become too attached to something or someone, we may develop a sense of possessiveness or entitlement that can harm others. For example, a parent who is overly attached to their child may try to control their child's life, leading to conflict and tension in the relationship. Similarly, a person who is attached to material possessions may become greedy or selfish, which can lead to negative consequences.

Attachment can also lead to suffering. When we attach ourselves to something or someone, we may experience anxiety, fear, or disappointment when we lose them or are separated from them. This can lead to a cycle of craving and aversion, which perpetuates negative *karma* and further suffering.

Therefore, it is important to cultivate non-attachment in our lives. Non-attachment does not mean detachment or apathy, but rather a sense of inner freedom and openness. When we let go of our attachment to things or people, we can experience greater peace, joy, and fulfillment. We can make decisions based on what is truly important to us and act in ways that are in alignment with our values and goals, rather than being driven by our attachments and desires.

Practicing mindfulness can help us become more aware of our attachments and develop a more non-attached approach to life. By observing our thoughts and emotions without judgment, we can become more grounded and present in the moment, and less reactive to our attachments and desires. Ultimately, non-attachment can lead to greater spiritual growth, positive *karma*, and inner peace.

In Buddhism, the concept of *tanha* refers to craving or thirst for something that one does not possess. This desire can manifest in various forms, such as a craving for material possessions, sensual pleasures, or even a craving for spiritual attainments. According to Buddhist teachings, *tanha* is one of the root causes of suffering, and its effects can be seen in the cycle of birth, death, and rebirth.

The desire for material possessions and sensual pleasures can lead to negative karmic consequences, such as greed, jealousy, and attachment. These negative emotions can cause one to act in unwholesome ways and accumulate negative *karma*. In turn, this negative *karma* can lead to further suffering and rebirth in lower realms.

Similarly, craving for spiritual attainments such as enlightenment can also lead to negative consequences. The desire for spiritual attainments can cause one to become attached to a particular idea or concept, leading to a narrow view of reality. This attachment can hinder spiritual growth and lead to spiritual stagnation.

The practice of Buddhism aims to overcome *tanha* through mindfulness and meditation. By developing mindfulness, one can become aware of their thoughts and emotions, and recognize the cravings and desires that arise within them. Through meditation, one can develop the ability to observe these desires without acting upon them, and eventually overcome them.

The concept of *tanha* in Buddhism highlights the dangers of craving and desire and their role in perpetuating suffering and negative *karma*. By becoming aware of these cravings and desires, and developing mindfulness and meditation, one can overcome them and achieve a state of inner peace and liberation.

Consumerism and materialism are two of the most significant factors that shape our desires and attachments in modern society. They drive the creation of wants and needs in individuals and reinforce the idea that happiness and satisfaction can be obtained through material possessions. In this way, consumerism and materialism can have a significant impact on our values and beliefs, shaping our desires and attachments toward material objects.

In many cases, the pursuit of material possessions leads to negative karmic consequences, such as greed, envy, and dissatisfaction. The constant craving for more material goods can lead to a never-ending cycle of desire, attachment, and negative *karma*. This can have a detrimental effect on our relationships, health, and overall well-being.

Furthermore, consumerism and materialism often encourage a "disposable" attitude towards possessions, leading to a lack of appreciation and gratitude for what we have. This can lead to feelings of emptiness and dissatisfaction, as well as negative karmic consequences.

Recognizing the impact of consumerism and materialism on our desires and attachments is crucial for those seeking to live a more mindful and spiritually aware life. By cultivating non-attachment and focusing on non-materialistic values, such as compassion and gratitude, individuals can break free from the negative karmic cycle of desire and attachment.

Ultimately, the path to reducing negative *karma* requires a conscious effort to examine our desires and attachments and to seek a deeper understanding of our values and beliefs. By recognizing and challenging the societal forces that shape our desires and attachments, we can cultivate a more mindful and compassionate approach to life, free from the negative karmic consequences of consumerism and materialism.

Detachment and non-attachment are central concepts in many spiritual practices, including Buddhism and Hinduism. These concepts emphasize the importance of letting go of attachments and desires to achieve a state of inner peace and spiritual liberation. By releasing our attachments, we can cultivate a sense of detachment from the material world and its fleeting pleasures, leading to a deeper sense of satisfaction and contentment. In the context of *karma*, attachment, and desire can lead to negative karmic consequences. When we are attached to certain outcomes or desires, we may act in ways that are not aligned with our *dharma*, leading to negative karmic consequences. By cultivating non-attachment and letting go of desires, we can act in ways that are more aligned with our higher purpose and positive karmic consequences.

Non-attachment and detachment can also help us navigate difficult situations with more ease and grace. <u>By letting go of our attachment to certain outcomes or expectations, we are better able to accept what is and find peace in the present moment.</u> This can be especially useful in times of change or uncertainty, where attachment to the past or fears about the future can cause unnecessary suffering.

In spiritual practices such as meditation, non-attachment is an important part of the process. By letting go of thoughts and attachments, we can access a deeper sense of stillness and inner peace. This can lead to greater self-awareness and a more profound sense of connection to the universe and others.

Overall, cultivating non-attachment and detachment can lead to greater inner peace and positive karmic consequences. By releasing our attachments and desires, we can act in ways that are more aligned with our higher purpose and spiritual growth.

In Hindu philosophy, the concept of *vasanas* refers to deep-seated desires and tendencies that shape our thoughts, emotions, and actions. These tendencies can be positive or negative, and they influence our personality, behavior, and ultimately our *karma*. According to Hinduism, *vasanas* are imprints from past lives that continue to affect our present life, shaping our likes, dislikes, and preferences.

Vasanas can be compared to habits or patterns of behavior that are deeply ingrained in our psyche. They are the result of our past actions and experiences, and they continue to influence our present and future actions. For example, if someone has a *vasana* for material possessions, they may be driven to accumulate wealth and material goods at the expense of other important aspects of life. On the other hand, if someone has a *vasana* for compassion and kindness, they may be inclined to help others and perform selfless acts.

While *vasanas* can have a positive influence on our lives, they can also lead to negative consequences if they are not balanced or controlled. Negative *vasanas* such as anger, greed, and envy can cause suffering and harm to oneself and others, perpetuating negative *karma*. Therefore, the goal of spiritual practice in Hinduism is to identify and transform negative *vasanas* into positive ones through self-awareness, self-reflection, and mindfulness.

By recognizing and transforming our *vasanas*, we can free ourselves from the cycle of birth and rebirth and achieve liberation or moksha. This requires a deep understanding of our own nature and a willingness to let go of negative tendencies and attachments. Through spiritual practices such as meditation, yoga, and self-inquiry, we can cultivate positive vasanas and reduce negative ones, leading to a more fulfilling and harmonious life.

Mindfulness is a state of present-moment awareness, where one is fully focused on the present experience without any judgment or distraction. In the context of desire and attachment, mindfulness can be an essential tool for recognizing and releasing them. By being present in the moment, individuals can become more aware of their thoughts, feelings, and sensations, and thus recognize the desires and attachments that may be driving their behavior.

Through mindfulness practice, individuals can learn to observe their desires and attachments without judgment or identification, which can help them release them. For instance, when one becomes aware of a desire for material possession or a particular outcome, one can take a moment to pause, observe the feeling, and release it without acting on it. With regular practice, mindfulness can help individuals develop the ability to let go of attachment and desire, leading to greater inner peace and freedom.

Moreover, mindfulness can also help individuals identify the underlying causes of their desires and attachments. Often, desires arise from a sense of lack or incompleteness, which can be addressed through self-reflection and inner work. By identifying the root cause of their desires and attachments, individuals can develop a deeper understanding of themselves and make conscious choices that align with their true values and aspirations.

In short, mindfulness can be a powerful tool for recognizing and releasing attachment and desire. Through regular practice, individuals can develop a greater awareness of their thoughts and emotions, identify the underlying causes of their desires, and make conscious choices that lead to greater inner peace and fulfillment.

Attachment and desire can have a profound impact on relationships and social dynamics. Attachment can arise from a deep emotional connection to someone or something, while desire may come from a longing or craving for something we do not have. In either case, attachment and desire can shape our actions and attitudes toward others.

When attachment and desire are positive and healthy, they can strengthen relationships and build social connections. However, when attachment and desire are negative and unhealthy, they can lead to suffering, conflict, and negative karmic consequences. For example, when someone is attached to their partner in an unhealthy way, they may become possessive or jealous, leading to a breakdown in trust and communication. In turn, this can cause suffering for both parties and negatively impact their *karma*.

Similarly, when desire is unchecked, it can lead to harmful behaviors that negatively impact relationships and social dynamics. For instance, when someone desires wealth or status above all else, they may engage in unethical or harmful behaviors to achieve their goals. This can harm others and negatively impact their *karma*.

Mindfulness can play a crucial role in recognizing and releasing unhealthy attachments and desires. By becoming aware of our thoughts, feelings, and actions, we can better understand how they impact our relationships and social dynamics. With this awareness, we can take steps to release negative attachments and desires, leading to positive relationships and social dynamics.

Overall, understanding the impact of attachment and desire on relationships and social dynamics is essential in living a life in line with *dharma* and positive *karma*. By cultivating healthy attachments and desires and releasing negative attachments and desires, individuals can lead fulfilling lives and positively impact those around them.

In Buddhism, one of the central teachings is the idea that attachment leads to suffering. This is because attachment creates an expectation that things will remain the same, which is not possible in a world of constant change. This is where the concept of *parinama-dukkha* comes into play. *Parinama-dukkha* refers to the suffering that arises from attachment and change. When we attach ourselves to things or people, we create a sense of dependency on them. We believe that they are necessary for our happiness and well-being. However, as everything in life is subject to change, we inevitably experience suffering when our attachments are disrupted.

For example, if we become attached to a certain job or career, we may experience great suffering if we lose that job or are forced to change careers. Similarly, if we become attached to a romantic partner, we may experience immense pain if the relationship ends.

However, the concept of *parinama-dukkha* is not meant to discourage attachment altogether. Instead, it is a reminder to approach attachment with mindfulness and non-attachment. By acknowledging the impermanence of all things and people, we can learn to appreciate them in the present moment without clinging to them.

Practicing non-attachment can help us to reduce suffering when changes inevitably occur. By releasing our attachment to things and people, we can find a greater sense of inner peace and freedom. Through mindfulness and self-reflection, we can cultivate a greater awareness of our attachments and work towards releasing them in a compassionate and loving way.

The New Age movement has gained widespread popularity in recent years with its focus on personal growth, spirituality, and self-improvement. A core belief within the movement is the law of attraction, which suggests that positive thoughts and intentions can manifest one's desires in life. However, this idea can become problematic when it is influenced by attachment and desire.

When individuals become attached to their desires and outcomes, they may become obsessed with manifesting their desires through the law of attraction. This attachment can lead to negative *karma*, as they may neglect ethical considerations and actions in the pursuit of their desires. Moreover, if the desired outcomes are not achieved, this can lead to disappointment, frustration, and even depression.

In the New Age movement, desire is often seen as a positive force that drives individuals toward their goals. However, the attachment to those desires can overshadow the importance of the journey towards those goals, including the lessons learned and the growth that comes with it. Additionally, attachment to desires can create a narrow focus, limiting the range of experiences and opportunities that an individual may encounter.

Therefore, it is important to practice detachment and mindfulness when manifesting desires through the law of attraction. Mindfulness can help individuals recognize their attachment to desires and work towards releasing them. Detachment can also help individuals stay grounded and connected to ethical considerations and actions in the pursuit of their desires.

The relationship between desire, attachment, and the law of attraction in the New Age movement can have a significant impact on an individual's karma. While the law of attraction can be a powerful tool for personal growth and transformation, it is important to approach it with mindfulness and detachment to avoid negative consequences.

CHAPTER 4

KARMA AND NATURAL LAW

One of the most intriguing aspects of *karma* and *dharma* is how they offer a unique perspective on the nature of suffering and adversity. In Hindu philosophy, suffering is seen as an inevitable aspect of the human experience, shaped by a complex interplay of *karma*, *dharma*, and the vagaries of fate. At the same time, the concept of *dharma* suggests that there is a duty or responsibility that accompanies every experience, including those that are difficult or painful. In this chapter, we will explore the nature of suffering in Hindu philosophy, examining how the principles of *karma* and *dharma* can help us understand and navigate difficult experiences. We will also explore the importance of compassion and resilience in the face of adversity and consider how we can cultivate a sense of spiritual purpose and meaning in the midst of even the most challenging circumstances.

The concept of karma is central to many Eastern philosophies and religions, including Hinduism, Buddhism, and Jainism. It refers to the idea that our actions have consequences that extend beyond our current lives, and that these consequences shape our future experiences. The word *karma* comes from the Sanskrit word *karman,* which means "action" or "deed".

According to the law of *karma*, every action we take, whether it be physical or mental, has a corresponding effect on our lives. Positive actions lead to positive consequences, while negative actions lead to negative consequences. *Karma* is often described as a kind of cosmic justice, in which individuals are held accountable for their actions and the impact they have on others.

Karma can be seen as a cycle, in which our actions create an energy that returns to us in the form of experiences, circumstances, and relationships. This cycle of cause and effect can continue over many lifetimes, with the actions of previous lives influencing our current experiences.

The concept of *karma* is closely related to the idea of *dharma*, or living in accordance with the natural order of the universe. Following *dharma* involves taking positive actions and making choices that align with our true nature and the greater good. By doing so, we can accumulate positive *karma* and improve our future experiences.

Understanding the concept of *karma* can help us become more mindful of our actions and the impact they have on ourselves and others. It can also help us to take responsibility for our choices and strive to make positive changes in our lives. Ultimately, the law of *karma* teaches us that we have the power to shape our future experiences through our thoughts, words, and actions.

In many spiritual traditions, including Buddhism and Hinduism, the concept of intention plays a crucial role in determining the karmic consequences of our actions. It is believed that the intention behind our actions is as important as the actions themselves, and that our intentions shape the nature and magnitude of the karmic energy that we generate.

For example, if we perform a seemingly good action, such as donating money to a charity, but our intention behind it is selfish or self-serving, the karmic consequences of that action may not be positive. On the other hand, if we perform a seemingly negative action, such as telling someone a hard truth, but our intention behind it is pure and compassionate, the karmic consequences may be positive.

The intention is also closely linked to mindfulness, which is the practice of being aware and present in the moment. By cultivating mindfulness, we can become more aware of our intentions and their impact on our actions and the world around us. This can help us to align our intentions with positive values and reduce the negative karmic consequences of our actions.

Moreover, understanding the role of intention in *karma* can also help us to take responsibility for our actions and the energy that we bring into the world. By becoming more conscious of our intentions, we can take steps to align them with positive values and generate more positive karma. This can lead to a more fulfilling and meaningful life, both for us and for those around us.

Karma is a fundamental concept in many Eastern religions and spiritual practices. It refers to the idea that our actions have consequences that can affect our present and future experiences. Understanding the difference between good and bad *karma* is important because it can help individuals make choices that lead to positive outcomes and avoid actions that lead to negative consequences.

Good karma is the result of positive actions, such as helping others, practicing generosity, and showing compassion. These actions are believed to create positive energy that can bring happiness, success, and fulfillment into our lives. Good *karma* is also said to create a sense of inner peace and contentment, as it aligns our actions with our values and beliefs.

In contrast, bad *karma* is the result of negative actions, such as harming others, being dishonest, or acting out of greed or selfishness. These actions are believed to create negative energy that can lead to suffering, unhappiness, and unfulfillment. Bad *karma* can also create a sense of guilt, regret, and inner turmoil, as it goes against our moral and ethical values.

Understanding the difference between good and bad *karma* can help individuals make choices that align with their values and goals. By choosing to act in ways that create positive energy, individuals can cultivate good *karma* and bring positivity into their lives. Additionally, by avoiding actions that create negative energy, individuals can avoid the negative consequences of bad *karma*.

In summary, understanding the difference between good and bad *karma* is essential for leading a fulfilling and meaningful life. By cultivating positive energy through good actions, individuals can create a sense of inner peace and contentment, while avoiding negative energy through bad actions can prevent unnecessary suffering and unhappiness.

The concept of past lives is central to many religious and spiritual beliefs, including Buddhism and Hinduism. According to these beliefs, our actions in past lives can have a significant impact on our current life and future, both in terms of our circumstances and our *karma*. This concept of past lives and its influence on *karma* is a complex and nuanced idea that has been debated and discussed for centuries.

In many spiritual traditions, the idea of reincarnation is closely tied to the concept of *karma*. The idea is that our actions in past lives can influence our current life and our future lives. If we have accumulated negative *karma* through our actions in past lives, we may experience negative consequences in our current life, and we may continue to accumulate negative *karma* that will affect our future lives. Conversely, if we have accumulated positive *karma* through our actions in past lives, we may experience positive consequences in our current life, and we may continue to accumulate positive *karma* that will affect our future lives.

The impact of past lives on *karma* is often difficult to understand and quantify, as it is based on complex metaphysical concepts that are beyond our current scientific understanding. However, the belief in past lives and *karma* can provide individuals with a framework for understanding the consequences of their actions and the importance of making ethical choices in their current life. It can also provide a sense of continuity and purpose to one's life, as the actions of one's current life are seen as having a ripple effect on one's past and future lives.

Many Eastern religions and philosophies believe in rebirth or reincarnation, which is the idea that after we die, our consciousness or soul is reborn into a new body. The concept of *karma* is closely tied to rebirth, as it is believed that our actions in this life can determine our rebirth and the experiences we will have in the next life.

According to this belief, our actions in this life create an accumulation of *karma*, which can have positive or negative consequences. If we live our lives with positive intentions and actions, we create positive *karma* that can lead to a better rebirth and a more positive experience in our next life. Conversely, negative actions and intentions can create negative *karma* that can lead to a less desirable rebirth and a more difficult experience in our next life.

The relationship between *karma* and rebirth is often described as a cycle, in which our actions in one life create the conditions for our experiences in the next life, and so on. This cycle can continue for many lifetimes until we reach a state of spiritual enlightenment or liberation, at which point we are no longer bound by the cycle of birth and rebirth.

The concept of *karma* and rebirth has significant implications for how individuals live their lives. It encourages individuals to take responsibility for their actions and to live in a way that is mindful of the consequences of those actions. It also encourages individuals to focus on personal growth and spiritual development, as the accumulation of positive *karma* can lead to a more positive and fulfilling experience in this life and future lives.

Meditation is an important practice in many spiritual traditions, including Buddhism and Hinduism, and can be a powerful tool for understanding and working with *karma*. Through meditation, individuals can cultivate greater awareness of their thoughts, feelings, and actions, and develop a deeper understanding of the relationship between cause and effect.

In meditation, individuals can learn to observe their thoughts and emotions without judgment, allowing them to identify patterns and habits that may be contributing to negative *karma*. For example, through meditation, one may become aware of a tendency to react impulsively to certain situations or to hold onto negative emotions such as anger or jealousy. By recognizing these patterns, individuals can begin to make changes in their behavior and develop more positive habits, leading to better *karma*.

Meditation can also help individuals cultivate positive qualities such as compassion, kindness, and generosity, which can in turn lead to positive *karma*. Through practices such as loving-kindness meditation, individuals can learn to extend these qualities to themselves and others, which can help create positive outcomes in their lives.

Another way that meditation can aid in understanding *karma* is by helping individuals develop a deeper sense of interconnectedness and interdependence. By recognizing how our actions affect others, and vice versa, individuals can become more aware of the consequences of their choices and work towards creating positive outcomes for themselves and those around them.

Overall, the practice of meditation can be a powerful tool for understanding and working with *karma*. By cultivating greater awareness and positive qualities, individuals can create positive *karma* and bring about positive changes in their lives and the lives of others.

The concept of *karma* has profound ethical implications. *Karma* refers to the law of cause and effect, where every action we take has a corresponding consequence. This means that our actions have the power to impact not only ourselves but also the world around us. In this sense, *karma* emphasizes the interconnectedness of all things and the importance of acting in an ethical and responsible manner.

The ethical implications of *karma* are rooted in the idea that our actions have consequences, and those consequences can either be positive or negative. If we act in a positive and ethical manner, we can create positive *karma*, which can lead to beneficial outcomes in our lives and the lives of those around us. On the other hand, if we act in a negative and unethical manner, we can create negative *karma*, which can lead to suffering and negative consequences.

Understanding the ethical implications of *karma* requires a deep understanding of the interconnectedness of all things. Our actions not only affect ourselves but also those around us, and the world. Thus, we must act in a way that is mindful of the impact our actions may have. This means acting in a way that promotes the well-being of us and others and avoiding actions that may cause harm.

The ethical implications of karma also emphasize the importance of personal responsibility. We cannot control the actions of others, but we can control our actions. Thus, it is up to us to act in a way that is positive and ethical and to take responsibility for the consequences of our actions.

In conclusion, the ethical implications of *karma* highlight the importance of acting in a way that is positive and ethical. By doing so, we can create positive *karma* and promote the well-being of ourselves and those around us. Understanding the interconnectedness of all things and taking personal responsibility for our actions is key to living a life that is mindful, ethical, and fulfilling.

In Hinduism, *dharma* refers to the duties, values, and behaviors that are in accordance with the natural order of the universe. It is considered one of the four aims of life, along with *artha* (material wealth), *kama* (pleasure), and *moksha* (liberation). *Dharma* is believed to be a guiding principle for individuals in living a fulfilling and purposeful life.

The concept of *karma* is closely related to *dharma*, as it refers to the law of cause and effect, where one's actions, thoughts, and intentions have consequences that can influence future experiences. *Karma* is based on the idea that one's present circumstances are the result of past actions, and one's future circumstances are influenced by present actions.

The relationship between *karma* and *dharma* is a complex one. While one's actions and intentions can influence their *karma*, the concept of *dharma* suggests that certain actions are considered more virtuous and in accordance with the natural order of the universe. Therefore, following one's *dharma* can lead to positive *karma*, as it involves fulfilling one's duties and living in alignment with the natural order of things.

However, it is important to note that the relationship between *karma* and *dharma* is not always straightforward. Sometimes, individuals may face difficult situations or have to make difficult choices that may not align with their *dharma*. In such cases, the intention behind the action may be more important than the action itself and can influence the karmic consequences.

The relationship between *karma* and *dharma* is a complex one, as it involves balancing one's actions and intentions with their duties and path in life. Understanding this relationship can help individuals live a more purposeful and fulfilling life, while also being mindful of the karmic consequences of their actions.

In Buddhism, *karma* is the concept that our actions and intentions have consequences that can impact our present and future experiences.

Positive actions and intentions lead to positive *karma*, while negative actions and intentions lead to negative *karma*. Mindfulness, or being aware and present in the moment, is an essential tool for creating positive karma.

Through mindfulness, we can become aware of our thoughts, emotions, and actions, and how they impact ourselves and others. By cultivating mindfulness, we can observe our behavior and ensure that our actions and intentions align with our values and beliefs. For example, if we are feeling angry, we can take a moment to pause and reflect on how we want to respond to the situation. By choosing a compassionate and constructive response, we can create positive *karma* and avoid negative consequences.

Additionally, mindfulness helps us to recognize the interconnectedness of all things. Our actions and intentions not only affect ourselves but also those around us and the world at large. By cultivating mindfulness, we can become more attuned to the impact of our actions and make choices that benefit the greater good. This includes being mindful of our consumption habits, how we treat others, and how we care for the environment.

Furthermore, mindfulness helps us to cultivate a sense of gratitude and appreciation for the present moment. By being mindful of the present, we can appreciate the opportunities and blessings that come our way, which can help us create positive *karma*. When we approach life with a sense of gratitude, we are more likely to act in ways that benefit ourselves and others, creating a positive cycle of *karma*.

<u>Overall, mindfulness is a powerful tool for creating positive karma.</u> By cultivating awareness and being present in the moment, we can align our actions and intentions with our values and beliefs, recognize the interconnectedness of all things, and appreciate the present moment.

Free Will - Action & In-Action

CHAPTER 5

THE POWER OF ACTION

*B*elief in fate or free-will action can vary among individuals and cultures. Some people believe that their lives are predetermined by fate or a higher power, while others believe that they have the power to shape their own lives through their choices and actions.

In many cultures, the concept of fate is deeply ingrained with the belief that everything happens for a reason and that events in one's life are predestined. This belief can bring a sense of comfort and acceptance, as it implies that there is a greater plan or purpose at work in the world. However, it can also lead to a sense of powerlessness and resignation, as individuals may feel that they have no control over the course of their lives.

On the other hand, the belief in free will emphasizes personal agency and responsibility. It suggests that individuals have the power to shape their own destinies through their choices and actions. This belief can be empowering, as it implies that individuals have the ability to create positive change in their lives and the world around them. However, it can also lead to feelings of guilt or self-blame if things do not go according to plan, as individuals may feel that they have failed to make the right choices or take the right actions.

Ultimately, whether individuals believe in fate or free will depends on a variety of factors, including their personal experiences, cultural background, and worldview.

Free will is a topic that has been debated for centuries, with philosophers, theologians, and scientists all offering different perspectives on the extent to which humans have the power to make choices that are truly free. At its core, free will is the ability to make choices that are not predetermined by external factors or influences, but rather reflect our own individual agency and autonomy. It is a fundamental aspect of human experience that underpins our sense of moral responsibility and personal accountability.

One of the key debates surrounding free will is the extent to which it is compatible with determinism, the idea that all events, including human actions, are ultimately determined by previous causes. Some argue that if determinism is true, then there can be no such thing as free will since all our choices would be predetermined by factors beyond our control. Others suggest that free will and determinism can coexist, since our actions may be determined by external factors, but we still have the ability to make choices within those constraints.

Another challenge to the idea of free will comes from the scientific study of the brain, which suggests that <u>our decisions may be influenced by unconscious processes that are beyond our conscious control.</u> For example, studies have shown that our brains begin to prepare for a decision before we are consciously aware of it, raising questions about the extent to which our choices are truly free.

Despite these challenges, many philosophers and theologians argue that free will is a necessary and essential aspect of human experience. They suggest that our ability to make choices that reflect our own values, desires, and aspirations is what gives our lives meaning and purpose and that without free will, we would be little more than passive observers of our own existence. Ultimately, the question of free will may never be fully resolved, but it remains a fascinating and deeply important topic for anyone interested in understanding the nature of human experience.

One best way to understand this is with an analogy of a cow tied to a tree, where the cow has free will to grace the lawn in and around the circumference and the length of the elastic rope depends on the good karma efforts & dharmic actions.

CHAPTER 6

THE POWER OF INACTION

*O*ne of the most intriguing aspects of *karma* and *dharma* is how they offer a distinctive perspective on the nature of action and inaction. In Hindu philosophy, the concept of karma suggests that all actions have consequences and that these consequences are shaped by a complex interplay of intention, context, and outcome. At the same time, the concept of *dharma* suggests that there is a duty or responsibility that accompanies every action and that this duty is shaped by a variety of factors, including social norms, personal values, and spiritual beliefs. In this chapter, we will explore the relationship between *karma* and *dharma*, examining how these concepts intersect and inform one another. We will also consider the implications of this relationship for our understanding of ethical decision-making, and for our broader sense of purpose and meaning in life.

The concept of action and inaction is a fundamental aspect of philosophy and plays a crucial role in understanding the concepts of *karma* and *dharma* too. According to Hinduism, every action has a consequence that affects an individual's spiritual journey, and the accumulation of these consequences over time is known as *karma*. However, not all actions lead to positive karmic consequences, and sometimes, inaction can be the better choice.

Inaction, in the context of karma and dharma, does not necessarily mean doing nothing. It means refraining from actions that may have negative karmic consequences or actions that do not align with dharma. Inaction can be a conscious choice made to avoid negative consequences, rather than a result of laziness or apathy.

The intention behind an action or inaction is also crucial in determining its karmic consequences. If an action is taken with the intention of harming others or with selfish motives, it is likely to lead to negative karmic consequences. Conversely, if an action is taken with the intention of helping others or with selfless motives, it is likely to lead to positive karmic consequences.

Furthermore, the concept of inaction also suggests that sometimes, it is better to let things be and trust in the natural order of things rather than trying to force outcomes. This can be seen in the Taoist concept of *wu wei*, which translates to *effortless action*. It suggests that by letting go of attachment to outcomes and surrendering to the present moment, one can achieve greater inner peace and clarity.

Overall, the concept of action and inaction in Hindu philosophy highlights the importance of mindfulness and intention in determining the karmic consequences of our actions. By making conscious choices that align with *dharma* and being mindful of our intentions, we can cultivate positive *karma* and progress on our spiritual journey.

In Hindu philosophy, *nishkama karma* refers to the performance of actions without attachment to the outcome. It is believed that when individuals perform actions without being attached to the outcome, they can achieve spiritual liberation. The concept of *nishkama karma* is rooted in the idea that attachment to the outcome of one's actions can lead to suffering and prevent individuals from achieving a state of inner peace and contentment.

Nishkama karma is often associated with the Bhagavad Gita, a Hindu scripture that explores the concept of *karma* and *dharma*. In the Bhagavad Gita, the protagonist Arjuna is faced with the dilemma of whether to fight a battle against his family members. Krishna, the god who advises Arjuna, tells him that he must perform his duty without attachment to the outcome and that the true goal of action is not the outcome but rather the purity of the action itself. Krishna explains that by performing actions without attachment to the outcome, one can achieve a state of equanimity and inner peace.

The concept of *nishkama karma* is not limited to Hinduism, as similar ideas can be found in other religious and philosophical traditions. For example, in Buddhism, the idea of non-attachment is central to the practice of mindfulness and meditation. The practice of non-attachment involves letting go of any attachment to thoughts, feelings, and sensations, and simply observing them without judgment or reaction.

In summary, the concept of *nishkama karma* emphasizes the importance of performing actions without attachment to the outcome. By letting go of attachment, individuals can achieve a state of inner peace and contentment, and ultimately move towards spiritual liberation.

<u>Non-violent resistance is a form of inaction that has been used as a powerful tool for change in social and political movements.</u> It is based on the principle of using peaceful means to resist oppression and injustice, rather than resorting to violence. Non-violent resistance seeks to challenge the status quo and bring about change through peaceful means such as civil disobedience, boycotts, and sit-ins.

The power of non-violent resistance lies in its ability to create a moral force that is difficult for oppressive regimes to resist. By refusing to resort to violence, non-violent resistance creates a powerful symbol of resistance that can galvanize public opinion and generate support from around the world. Non-violent resistance has been used throughout history to challenge oppressive regimes and bring about social and political change, from Gandhi's campaign of non-cooperation against British rule in India to the Civil Rights Movement in the United States.

Non-violent resistance can also be an effective means of bringing about change without resorting to violence. It can be a way to challenge entrenched power structures and bring about change through peaceful means. Non-violent resistance can also be used to create space for dialogue and negotiation, as it provides a means of challenging the status quo without resorting to violence.

However, non-violent resistance is not without its risks. It requires a great deal of courage and sacrifice from those involved, as they may face arrest, imprisonment, or even violence from the authorities. Non-violent resistance also requires a high degree of organization and discipline, as well as a clear strategy and goal.

Despite these challenges, non-violent resistance remains a powerful tool for change in social and political movements. It provides a means of challenging oppressive regimes and bringing about change through peaceful means, while also creating a powerful symbol of resistance that can inspire others around the world.

Mindfulness is the practice of being present in the moment and paying attention to one's thoughts, feelings, and surroundings without judgment. It can be practiced through techniques such as meditation, yoga, or simply by being fully present in daily activities. In the context of inaction, mindfulness can play a crucial role in helping individuals make more conscious and effective choices.

By practicing mindfulness, individuals can become more aware of their own motivations and intentions. This awareness can help them identify whether their actions are driven by ego or a genuine desire to do good. Additionally, mindfulness can help individuals identify when action is necessary and when inaction may be the best course of action. It can help them become more attuned to their surroundings and recognize when intervention is necessary, and when it is better to let things unfold naturally.

Furthermore, mindfulness can help individuals cultivate a greater sense of inner peace and clarity. This can help them approach difficult situations with a clear mind and heart, which can lead to more effective action when action is necessary. By staying present and grounded in the moment, individuals can avoid getting caught up in anxieties about the future or regrets about the past and instead focus on what needs to be done in the present moment.

The practice of mindfulness can be a powerful tool in the practice of inaction. By cultivating greater self-awareness and clarity, individuals can make more conscious choices that align with their values and lead to positive karmic consequences.

The dangers of inaction are evident in situations where social justice and environmental issues are at stake. In such cases, inaction can lead to the perpetuation of existing problems, or even make them worse. For instance, if a society fails to take action against discrimination, it can lead to the marginalization of certain groups, which can have long-lasting effects on their well-being and opportunities. Similarly, if people fail to act on environmental issues such as climate change, it can lead to irreversible damage to the planet, affecting future generations.

Inaction can stem from various reasons, such as a lack of awareness or understanding of the issue, a feeling of helplessness, or simply not wanting to get involved. However, it is important to recognize that inaction can lead to negative consequences and that action is often necessary to bring about positive change.

Individuals and communities can take action in different ways to address social and environmental issues. This can include speaking up against injustice, participating in peaceful protests or demonstrations, supporting organizations or initiatives that work towards positive change, or making changes in one's personal life to reduce environmental impact.

While it may seem overwhelming to take on such issues, it is important to remember that even small actions can have an impact. In fact, collective action often leads to greater change than individual action. By taking a step toward action, individuals can become part of a larger movement toward positive change and help create a more just and sustainable future.

The role of surrender in the practice of inaction, and how letting go of attachment to outcomes can lead to greater inner peace:

The concept of surrender in the context of inaction is closely related to the concept of detachment. Detachment refers to the state of being unattached to the outcome of an action, allowing for a sense of inner peace and freedom from suffering. Surrender takes detachment a step further, as it involves not only letting go of attachment to outcomes but also surrendering oneself completely to a higher power or divine will.

In Hindu philosophy, surrender is referred to as *prapatti*, which means self-surrender or complete surrender. This concept is closely related to the idea of bhakti, or devotion to a divine being. Surrendering to a higher power allows one to let go of their ego and the sense of control over their life, leading to a deeper sense of peace and connection to the divine.

In the context of inaction, surrender involves letting go of attachment to the outcome of an action and trusting in the universe or a higher power to guide the situation. It allows for a sense of freedom from anxiety and stress that can come from trying to control everything in one's life. Surrendering can also lead to a greater sense of acceptance and contentment with one's life circumstances.

Overall, the practice of surrender in the context of inaction can be a powerful tool for achieving inner peace and spiritual growth. By letting go of attachment to outcomes and surrendering to a higher power, individuals can find a sense of freedom from suffering and a deeper connection to the divine.

The Taoist concept of *wu wei*, or effortless action, is about finding a balance between action and inaction, effort and ease. It is about letting go of the ego-driven need to constantly strive and achieve, and instead surrendering to the flow of life. By embracing this concept, we can tap into a deeper sense of purpose and meaning and live a life that is more in harmony with our true nature.

In today's fast-paced society, we often prioritize action over stillness, valuing productivity and output above all else. However, this constant need to be "doing something" can actually hinder our creativity and limit our potential for innovation. Taking a step back from action and practicing inaction can provide the space and clarity necessary to unlock new ideas and solutions.

When we engage in non-action, we create a void in which new ideas can arise. By intentionally stepping away from the busyness of everyday life and giving ourselves the time and space to reflect, we tap into a deeper well of creativity and inspiration. In this way, inaction can be seen as an essential component of the creative process.

Inaction can also help to break us out of habitual patterns of thinking and behaving, allowing us to approach problems and challenges from a new perspective. By letting go of our attachment to outcomes and surrendering to the present moment, we free ourselves from the limitations of our own thinking and open ourselves up to new possibilities.

Inaction can take many forms, from meditation and mindfulness practices to simply taking a break from our daily routine. Regardless of the form it takes, the power of inaction lies in its ability to provide us with the space and clarity necessary to tap into our innate creativity and unlock our full potential. By prioritizing stillness and taking intentional breaks from action, we can cultivate a deeper sense of inspiration, innovation, and meaning in our lives.

The concept of *right action* is an important aspect of Buddhist philosophy, which emphasizes the importance of ethical behavior and morality in achieving enlightenment. *Right action* refers to actions that are in line with the Buddha's teachings and contribute to the well-being of oneself and others. However, in some cases, *right action* may also involve inaction or non-doing.

Inaction can be a powerful tool in spiritual practice, particularly in the context of mindfulness and meditation. In mindfulness meditation, practitioners are encouraged to simply observe their thoughts and sensations without judgment or action. By practicing non-reactivity and non-attachment to one's thoughts and emotions, individuals can cultivate greater awareness and inner peace.

Similarly, in some forms of meditation, practitioners may focus on cultivating a sense of emptiness or non-doing, rather than actively engaging in mental or physical activity. This can help individuals let go of attachment to outcomes and cultivate a sense of inner calm and detachment.

In the context of *right action*, inaction may also involve refraining from harmful actions, such as lying, stealing, or harming others. By avoiding harmful actions, individuals can contribute to the well-being of themselves and others and avoid negative karmic consequences.

Overall, the concept of *right action* emphasizes the importance of ethical behavior and morality in achieving enlightenment, but also recognizes the potential power of inaction in spiritual practice. By practicing non-reactivity, non-attachment, and refraining from harmful actions, individuals can cultivate greater awareness, inner peace, and positive karmic consequences.

In Buddhism, the concept of *right action* is one of the components of the Noble Eightfold Path, which is the path to enlightenment. It refers to the idea that one should engage in ethical conduct and avoid harmful behavior. However, sometimes the right action may be inaction. This means that sometimes refraining from taking action is the appropriate choice, particularly in situations where taking action may cause harm or lead to negative consequences.

The practice of inaction as a form of *right action* is particularly relevant in situations where one's actions may have negative consequences for others, such as in issues of social justice or political conflict. By refraining from taking action that may cause harm, individuals can work towards resolving these issues in a way that is respectful and mindful of all parties involved.

The concept of *right action* can also be applied to daily life. For example, if one is feeling overwhelmed or stressed, taking a step back and refraining from action can be the right choice. This can allow for reflection, self-awareness, and a better understanding of how to move forward in a positive way.

<u>Ultimately, the practice of inaction as a form of right action requires a deep understanding of one's intentions and motivations.</u> By being mindful and self-reflective, individuals can make choices that align with their values and beliefs, while also taking into account the impact of their actions on others.

CHAPTER 7

THE POWER OF THE SECOND-BEST OPTION

*I*n many cultures, the pursuit of excellence is viewed as a fundamental aspect of the human experience, driving us to achieve our full potential and reach new heights of accomplishment. In the Hindu tradition, this pursuit is deeply connected to the concept of *karma*, which suggests that the quality of our actions has a direct impact on the quality of our lives. At the same time, the concept of *dharma* suggests that there is a duty or responsibility that accompanies every action and that this duty must be balanced against our desire for excellence. In this chapter, we will explore the relationship between excellence and duty in Hindu philosophy, examining how these concepts can help us cultivate a sense of purpose and meaning in our lives. We will also explore the importance of humility and compassion in the pursuit of excellence and consider how we can use the principles of *karma* and *dharma* to cultivate a sense of balance and equanimity in our quest for greatness.

The concept of the second-best option can be a difficult one to accept, as many people strive for perfection and believe that settling for anything less is a failure. However, this concept emphasizes the idea that the second-best option can still lead to positive outcomes and opportunities for growth.

Understanding the second-best option can be applied to various aspects of life, including career choices, relationships, and personal goals. For example, if someone does not get their first-choice job, they may be offered a second-choice job that still aligns with their values and provides opportunities for growth. In this scenario, it is important to recognize the positive aspects of the second-choice job and focus on how it can lead to further career opportunities and development.

This concept can also be applied to personal goals and aspirations. For example, if someone's dream is to write a novel but they are struggling to find the time or motivation, they may need to consider a second-best option, such as writing shorter pieces or taking a writing course. The second-best option can still provide valuable experience and lead to growth as a writer.

Overall, understanding the concept of the second-best option can lead to a more flexible and adaptable mindset, where individuals can appreciate the opportunities and growth that can arise from accepting and embracing alternative paths to their goals.

The concept of the second-best option highlights the idea that sometimes the ideal choice may not be available or practical, and in such cases, we must settle for the next best alternative. This idea raises the question of how we can make the most of the options available to us and choose the second-best option in the most effective way possible.

Effective decision-making is crucial in selecting the second-best option. This concept requires an individual to be aware of their priorities and values and have a clear understanding of their goals. One decision-making strategy that can help is weighing the pros and cons of each option and determining which alternative best aligns with their values and objectives. Another strategy is considering the potential consequences of each choice and the impact it will have in the long run.

Individuals can also benefit from a growth mindset, which involves embracing challenges and being open to new opportunities. This mindset allows individuals to recognize that the second-best option may present a unique opportunity for growth and development. Moreover, it's important to approach the second-best option with a positive attitude and an open mind. This can lead to a more optimistic outlook, which can have a significant impact on the outcome.

It's also crucial to acknowledge that the second-best option may not always be a compromise or a "lesser" option. Instead, it can be an opportunity for exploration and discovery. By exploring different options, individuals can discover new paths that they may have otherwise overlooked.

Lastly, individuals can benefit from learning to let go of the fear of missing out and embrace the idea of *good enough*. This approach involves recognizing that perfection is often unattainable, and sometimes, the second-best option can be a satisfactory and fulfilling choice. In summary, the role of decision-making in choosing the second-best option is critical, and effective decision-making strategies can help individuals make the most of the options available to them.

The concept of the second-best option is rooted in the idea that sometimes in life, we may not always achieve our first choice or desired outcome. In these instances, we are presented with a second-best option, which can be an alternative path to achieving our goals. This idea explores the connection between acceptance and choosing the second-best option. It examines how acceptance can play a vital role in helping individuals embrace the opportunities presented by the second-best option.

<u>Acceptance is the act of acknowledging and coming to terms with the reality of a situation.</u> It involves embracing the present moment and recognizing that we cannot change what has already happened. Acceptance allows us to move forward from disappointment and focus

on the opportunities presented to us. In the context of the second-best option, acceptance can be the key to choosing this alternative path. <u>It involves letting go of attachment to the original desired outcome and embracing the potential of the second-best option.</u>

Choosing the second-best option can be a challenging decision, as it may involve letting go of a dream or goal. However, acceptance can make this decision easier by helping individuals to recognize the potential of the second-best option. By accepting the reality of the situation, individuals can focus on the opportunities presented by the alternative path, rather than dwelling on what could have been.

Acceptance can also help individuals to approach the second-best option with an open mind and a positive attitude. By letting go of attachment to the original desired outcome, individuals can approach the alternative path with curiosity and excitement, recognizing the potential for growth and learning. This can lead to a more fulfilling journey and a greater sense of satisfaction in the long run.

The connection between acceptance and the second-best option is a powerful one. By accepting the reality of a situation, individuals can move forward from disappointment and embrace the opportunities presented by the alternative path. This can lead to personal growth, learning, and a more fulfilling journey toward achieving one's goals.

We tend to view the second-best option as a compromise or a fallback option and may feel disappointed or dissatisfied with it. However, by shifting our perspective, we can begin to appreciate the value of the second-best option and find joy in the opportunities it presents. Also one can learn from the person who accomplished the first option and try further when the opportunity comes, maybe the effort required could be less than the person who suggested getting the first option because we learned from that first-timer who accomplished it the hard way.

One way to shift our perspective is to focus on the positive aspects of the second-best option. Instead of thinking about what we're missing out on by not choosing the ideal option, we can focus on what we gain from the second-best option. This could be an opportunity to learn something new, to challenge ourselves in a different way, or to explore a new avenue that we may not have considered otherwise.

Another way to shift our perspective is to reframe our thinking about the situation. Instead of seeing the second-best option as a compromise, we can view it as a stepping stone toward our ultimate goal. By taking advantage of the opportunities presented by the second-best option, we can build our skills, knowledge, and experience, which can help us achieve our long-term goals.

Finally, practicing gratitude can also help shift our perspective. By focusing on what we're grateful for in the second-best option, we can cultivate a sense of appreciation for the opportunities it presents. This can help us find joy and satisfaction in the present moment, even if it's not exactly what we had hoped for.

Overall, the impact of perspective on the second-best option is significant. By shifting our perspective and focusing on the positive aspects of the second-best option, we can find joy, satisfaction, and opportunities for growth and development.

In life, we are often faced with difficult decisions where we have to choose between different options. We may have a clear idea of what we want, but circumstances may not allow us to pursue our first choice. This is where the concept of the second-best option comes in. The second-best option refers to choosing an option that is not our first choice, but one that is still satisfactory and can lead to positive outcomes.

Choosing the second-best option can be a valuable opportunity for personal growth and development. It can help us develop resilience, flexibility, and adaptability. When we are faced with situations where we cannot have our first choice, we have the opportunity to challenge ourselves and embrace new experiences. We learn how to navigate through uncertainty and become more comfortable with change.

Additionally, choosing the second-best option can also help us discover new interests and passions that we may not have explored otherwise. It can open doors to new opportunities and help us broaden our perspectives. When we are willing to embrace the second-best option, we can also develop a sense of gratitude and appreciation for what we have. This can lead to greater contentment and happiness in life.

However, it's important to note that embracing the second-best option does not mean settling for less or compromising our values. It means accepting that sometimes circumstances do not allow us to have everything we want and that it's okay to make the best of what we have. By doing so, we can grow and develop in ways we may not have expected and find fulfillment in the journey.

The concept of *good enough* challenges the notion that only the best outcome is acceptable. It suggests that sometimes the second-best option can be sufficient and even preferable in certain situations. The idea behind this concept is to avoid the trap of perfectionism, which can lead to missed opportunities, delays, and an inability to move forward.

In practice, the concept of *good enough* can help individuals make more efficient and effective decisions by focusing on the most practical and realistic options available. By accepting that not everything will be perfect, individuals can be more proactive and take action when they have a good opportunity that meets their basic requirements.

This concept is particularly relevant in today's fast-paced world, where there is often a sense of urgency and pressure to achieve the best outcomes. By accepting "good enough" as a valid option, individuals can avoid getting stuck in a cycle of overthinking and procrastination, which can lead to missed opportunities.

However, it is important to note that "good enough" should not be used as an excuse for mediocrity or for settling for less than what one deserves. Rather, it is about recognizing when the second-best option is truly sufficient and not getting too caught up in the pursuit of perfection.

Ultimately, the concept of *good enough* encourages individuals to let go of the idea of perfection and instead focus on taking action and making progress toward their goals. By being more flexible and open-minded, individuals can achieve more positive outcomes and avoid unnecessary stress and frustration.

The concept of the second-best option is based on the idea that sometimes, our first choice may not always be available or may not be the best option for us in the long run. In such cases, the second-best option may offer us a better outcome than sticking to our original choice. However, fear can often prevent us from embracing the second-best option, even if it offers us a greater potential for growth and fulfillment.

This idea explores the different types of fear that can impact our decision-making process when faced with the second-best option. For instance, we may fear failure, uncertainty, or the judgment of others. These fears can make us hesitant to choose the second-best option, as we may be afraid of the potential consequences or unknown outcomes.

Overcoming these fears is crucial for embracing the second-best option and making the most of it. This may involve examining our beliefs and assumptions about success and failure and recognizing that failure is often an opportunity for growth and learning. It may also involve cultivating a sense of curiosity and openness to new experiences, even if they may be unfamiliar or uncomfortable.

Another aspect of this concept is recognizing the potential benefits of the second-best option. While it may not be our ideal choice, it may offer us opportunities for personal growth, new experiences, and unexpected benefits that we may not have considered otherwise.

Overall, this concept emphasizes the importance of confronting our fears and biases to embrace the potential of the second-best option. By recognizing the potential benefits and reframing our perspective on success and failure, we can make the most of the opportunities presented to us, even if they may not be our first choice.

The concept of the second-best option refers to choosing an alternative option when the ideal or first choice is unavailable. This idea recognizes that sometimes in life, we may not be able to achieve our ideal outcome, but we can still find value and happiness in the second-best option.

Gratitude plays an essential role in making the most of the second-best option. When we practice gratitude, we cultivate an appreciation for what we have rather than focusing on what we don't have. This mindset shift can help us see the benefits and opportunities of the second-best option.

Furthermore, practicing gratitude can help us find joy in unexpected places. When we are grateful, we are more open to the possibilities and opportunities presented by the second-best option. We can shift our perspective and look for the positive aspects of the situation, rather than dwelling on what we have lost.

In addition, gratitude can help us build resilience and cope with disappointment. When we focus on what we are grateful for, we build a sense of internal strength that can help us face challenging situations. We can draw on this strength to make the most of the second-best option and move forward with a positive outlook.

Overall, the role of gratitude in the second-best option highlights the importance of cultivating a mindset of appreciation and positivity. By focusing on what we have and being grateful for it, we can find joy and fulfillment in unexpected places and make the most of the opportunities presented by the second-best option.

Choosing the second-best option is often seen as settling for something that is not ideal or perfect. However, this concept explores how choosing the second-best option can actually contribute to resilience. Resilience refers to an individual's ability to adapt to change and overcome obstacles. It involves being flexible and open to new possibilities, even if they are not what we initially hoped for.

Choosing the second-best option can be seen as a form of resilience because it involves making the most of the resources and opportunities available to us, even if they are not our first choice. It requires us to be adaptable and open-minded, which are key traits of resilience. Rather than giving up or becoming discouraged when our first choice is not available, we can learn to embrace the second-best option and make the most of it.

Additionally, choosing the second-best option can help us develop a sense of gratitude and appreciation for what we have. When we focus too much on what we don't have or what we can't have, it can lead to feelings of disappointment and frustration. However, when we focus on the second-best option and how we can make it work for us, we can develop a sense of gratitude and appreciation for what we do have. This can help us cultivate a more positive mindset and improve our overall well-being.

Overall, this concept explores how choosing the second-best option can contribute to resilience by fostering adaptability, openness, and gratitude. Rather than seeing it as settling or giving up, we can learn to embrace the second-best option as an opportunity to grow and thrive.

In our society, there is often a lot of pressure to pursue certain goals or outcomes that are deemed "successful" or "prestigious". These can include getting a high-paying job, owning a big house, or achieving a certain level of education. As a result, many people feel like they must always choose the "best" option, even if it's not what they truly want or need.

This pressure to conform to societal expectations can make it difficult for individuals to choose the second-best option, even when it might be a better fit for them. For example, someone might feel like they need to pursue a certain career path because it's seen as more prestigious, even though they might be happier and more fulfilled in a different field that is considered less prestigious.

Choosing the second-best option can also come with feelings of disappointment or failure, especially if it feels like settling for less than what we really wanted. This can be particularly challenging when we are comparing ourselves to others who have achieved what we thought was the "best" option.

However, it's important to remember that the second-best option can still be a good choice, and even lead to positive outcomes. <u>It's important to listen to our own needs and desires, rather than solely focusing on external expectations.</u> This can allow us to choose a path that is better suited for us, even if it doesn't align with what society considers "successful".

Ultimately, the second-best option can be a valuable opportunity for growth and self-discovery. It can allow us to explore new paths, learn new skills, and develop a greater sense of self-awareness. By embracing the second-best option, we can learn to prioritize our own well-being and happiness, rather than external expectations.

Dharma - Right & Virtue

CHAPTER 8

DHARMA IN ACTION

*T*he concept of *dharma* is a central tenet of philosophy and is often described as the underlying moral and ethical order of the universe. While *dharma* is a complex and multifaceted concept, at its core, it is concerned with the idea of right action – that is, acting in accordance with the moral and ethical principles that govern our lives. In this chapter, we will explore the concept of *dharma* in action, examining how it can guide our decision-making processes, and shape the way we engage with the world around us. We will also consider the role that *dharma* plays in our pursuit of personal and spiritual fulfillment and explore how it can help us cultivate a sense of purpose, meaning, and compassion in our lives. To understand *dharma*, its relation to various aspects of our life is important.

The concept of *dharma* is there in both Hinduism and Buddhism, which refers to the natural order of the universe and one's duty or purpose in life. There are some slightly different interpretations of *dharma* in both religions and how it is related to *karma*, reincarnation, and liberation from the cycle of rebirth.

In Hinduism, *swadharma* refers to one's individual duty or purpose in life. This refers to one's individual duty or purpose in life. It explores how individuals can discover their *swadharma* and how fulfilling it can lead to a sense of fulfillment and happiness. The importance of mindfulness in fulfilling one's *dharma* is about the role of mindfulness in fulfilling one's *dharma*. It discusses how being present and aware of one's actions and intentions can help individuals align with their duty or purpose in life and create positive *karma*. The impact of ego and attachment on fulfilling one's dharma is about the impact of ego and attachment on fulfilling one's *dharma*. It deals with how attachment to outcomes and desires can lead to conflict with one's duty or purpose in life, and how individuals can overcome these obstacles. The concept of *karma yoga* in Hinduism refers to the path of action and service as a means to spiritual growth and enlightenment. It examines how this concept is rooted in the idea of selfless service and detachment from the fruits of one's actions, and how it can be applied in daily life to cultivate a sense of purpose and meaning.

In Buddhism, the concept of *right livelihood* refers to ethical and meaningful work. It explores how individuals can align their careers with their *dharma* and how fulfilling work can lead to a sense of fulfillment and purpose. The role of service and altruism is about fulfilling one's dharma. It discusses how acts of service and compassion can help individuals fulfill their duty or purpose in life and create positive *karma*. The concept of *upaya* in Buddhism refers to skillful means or strategies used to help others achieve enlightenment. It examines how this concept is connected to the idea of compassion and how it can be applied in daily life to help others.

The concept of *ahimsa* in Hinduism and Buddhism refers to non-violence and the avoidance of harm to others. It examines how this concept is connected to *dharma* and how it can be applied in daily life to cultivate a sense of peace and compassion.

The concept of *seva* in Sikhism refers to selfless service to others. It examines how this concept is connected to *dharma* and how it can be applied in daily life to cultivate a sense of humility and compassion.

The importance of self-reflection in understanding and fulfilling one's dharma examines the importance of self-reflection in understanding and fulfilling one's *dharma*. It discusses how individuals can reflect on their values, desires, and actions to better align with their duty or purpose in life and create positive change.

The importance of aligning one's actions with their dharma to find fulfillment and meaning in life is about how living in accordance with one's dharma can lead to a sense of purpose and a deeper understanding of oneself.

<u>The role of self-discovery and introspection in identifying one's dharma is about the importance of understanding one's strengths, weaknesses, and passions in defining one's purpose and dharma.</u>

Understanding the connection between *dharma* and the greater good is vital. It explores how living in accordance with one's *dharma* can lead to positive impacts and contributions to society.

The impact of external factors, such as financial stability or societal pressures, on living in accordance with one's *dharma* is critical for balancing practical considerations with one's true purpose.

The role of mentorship and guidance in finding and living in accordance with one's *dharma* is related to seeking guidance from others that can provide valuable insights and support in pursuing one's purpose.

The potential challenges and obstacles that may arise when living in accordance with one's *dharma* and strategies for overcoming them determine the importance of perseverance and resilience in pursuing one's true purpose.

The importance of non-attachment in fulfilling one's *dharma* explores the importance of non-attachment in fulfilling one's *dharma*. It deals with how attachment can lead to negative *karma* and hinder one's ability to fulfill their life purpose.

<u>Societal expectations on an individual's ability have a direct impact on the individual to pursue their personal dharma, and it is important to break free from these expectations to live a fulfilling life.</u>

The role of social and cultural expectations in shaping one's understanding of *dharma* portrays how social and cultural expectations can impact an individual's understanding of their *dharma*.

Understanding the relationship between dharma and personal growth is about living in alignment with one's purpose which can lead to personal growth and development, and how personal growth can help individuals better understand and fulfill their dharma.

The role of service in fulfilling one's dharma is about how using one's talents and abilities to serve others can bring about a sense of purpose and fulfillment.

The impact of fear and limiting beliefs on living in alignment with one's dharma is about the impact of fear and limiting beliefs on living in alignment with one's *dharma*. It deals with the importance of overcoming these obstacles and trusting in one's purpose to create positive *karma* and fulfillment.

The role of compassion in dharma is about how cultivating compassion can help individuals live in alignment with their *dharma* and contribute to the greater good.

The concept of *karma phala* or the fruits of one's actions relates to the pursuit of *dharma*: It is about how pursuing *dharma*, or righteous living, can lead to positive *karma phala* and a fulfilling life.

Understanding the impact of intention and motivation in pursuing *dharma* is about how having pure intentions and a genuine desire to do good can lead to positive karma and a deeper connection to one's spiritual path.

The role of meditation and introspection in understanding one's dharma is about how taking the time to reflect on one's values, desires, and motivations can lead to a deeper understanding of one's personal duty and path.

The role of *karma yoga* or selfless action in pursuing *dharma* is about how acting selflessly and without attachment to the fruits of one's actions can lead to positive *karma* and a deeper connection to one's spiritual path.

Understanding the importance of balance and moderation in pursuing *dharma* is about the importance of balance and moderation in pursuing *dharma*. It is a balancing act on how avoiding extremes and finding a middle path can lead to positive *karma* and a fulfilling life.

The relationship between *dharma* and social justice is about the relationship between *dharma* and social justice. It emphasizes how fulfilling one's duty or purpose in life can contribute to creating a just and equitable society, and how individuals can use their *dharma* to create positive change in the world.

CHAPTER 9

DHARMA AND SOCIAL JUSTICE

*I*n Hindu philosophy, the concept of *karma* extends beyond the realm of personal morality and encompasses our relationship with the natural world. The way we treat the environment is seen as a reflection of our moral and spiritual values, and our actions can have far-reaching karmic consequences. In this chapter, we will explore the relationship between *karma* and the environment, examining how our actions impact the natural world and how we can cultivate a more compassionate and sustainable relationship with the planet. We will also consider how environmental degradation and climate change are connected to broader issues of social justice and explore the role of *karma* in addressing these global challenges.

The impact of social and cultural factors on fulfilling one's *dharma* is about how social and cultural factors can impact an individual's ability to fulfill their *dharma*. Our societal expectations and cultural norms can conflict with one's duty or purpose in life, and one must know how to navigate these challenges.

The concept of *karma* in Hindu philosophy suggests that our actions and intentions have far-reaching consequences, not just for ourselves and others, but also for the environment. The way we treat the natural world is seen as a reflection of our moral and spiritual values, and our actions can have a profound impact on the health and well-being of the planet.

The interconnectedness of all life forms and natural systems is a central tenet of Hindu philosophy, and this perspective is reflected in the concept of *karma*. Every action we take has a ripple effect that extends far beyond ourselves, impacting the lives of other beings and the natural world as a whole. When we act in harmony with the natural world, we create positive karmic consequences that benefit all living beings. When we act in ways that harm the environment, we create negative karmic consequences that can have serious implications for future generations.

The degradation of the environment and the looming threat of climate change are among the most pressing issues the world faces today, and they are inextricably linked to issues of social justice and human well-being. The concept of *karma* can provide a useful lens through which to understand and address these challenges. By recognizing the interconnectedness of all life and the importance of acting in ways that are aligned with our moral and spiritual values, we can begin to cultivate a more compassionate and sustainable relationship with the planet.

One way to apply the principles of *karma* to our relationship with the environment is through the practice of *ahimsa*, or non-violence. This principle holds that we should strive to do no harm to any living being, including the natural world. By reducing our ecological footprint, conserving resources, and supporting sustainable practices, we can help to create positive karmic consequences that benefit both ourselves and future generations.

Another way to apply the principles of *karma* to environmental issues is through the practice of *seva*, or selfless service. This principle encourages us to act in service to others and the natural world, recognizing that our actions have the power to create positive change. By engaging in environmental activism, supporting conservation efforts, and working to address climate change, we can create positive karmic consequences that benefit all living beings.

The concept of *dharma* can provide a useful framework for understanding our relationship with the environment and for addressing the pressing environmental challenges facing the world today. By recognizing the interconnectedness of all life and the importance of acting in ways that are aligned with our moral and spiritual values, we can begin to cultivate a more compassionate and sustainable relationship with the planet, creating positive karmic consequences that benefit all living beings.

Social justice is a pressing concern in today's world, as we grapple with issues of inequality, discrimination, and marginalization on a global scale. In Hindu philosophy, the concept of *dharma* plays a key role in shaping our understanding of social justice, suggesting that our actions and intentions have a profound impact on the well-being of others and the larger social fabric. In this chapter, we will explore the concept of *dharma* in relation to social justice, examining how it is related to issues of equality, human rights, and social responsibility. We will also consider the implications of this idea for our understanding of politics, economics, and social change, and explore how it can help us create a more just and equitable world for all.

Social justice is a complex and multifaceted issue, encompassing a range of concerns related to equality, human rights, and social responsibility. In Hindu philosophy, the concept of *dharma* offers a framework for understanding these issues, suggesting that our actions and intentions have a profound impact on the well-being of others and the larger social fabric. *Dharma* refers to our duty or purpose in life and suggests that we have a responsibility to act in accordance with our moral principles and spiritual values.

When we apply these principles to the issue of social justice, we can see that *dharma* is closely related to issues of equality, human rights, and social responsibility. For example, if we recognize our duty to treat others with respect, empathy, and compassion, we are more likely to advocate for their rights and well-being and to oppose systems of oppression and discrimination. Similarly, if we recognize our responsibility to act in accordance with our values and principles, we are more likely to engage in social and political action that promotes justice, equality, and human dignity.

This idea has important implications for our understanding of politics, economics, and social change. If we view these issues solely in terms of power and self-interest, we may overlook the importance of our moral and spiritual values in shaping our actions and intentions. However, if we view them in terms of *dharma*, we can see how our values and principles can guide us toward more just and equitable outcomes.

For example, in the realm of economics, we can see how the concept of dharma can guide us toward a more equitable distribution of resources and opportunities. Rather than viewing wealth and power as ends in themselves, we can see them as means to promote the well-being of all members of society. Similarly, in the realm of politics, we can see how the concept of *dharma* can guide us toward policies and practices that promote human dignity, freedom, and equality, rather than simply serving the interests of those in power.

Ultimately, the concept of *dharma* offers a powerful tool for promoting social justice, by recognizing our responsibility to act in accordance with our values and principles. By recognizing the interconnectedness of all beings, and the impact of our actions and intentions on the larger social fabric, we can work towards a more just and equitable world for all.

Virtue and *dharma* are closely connected concepts in Hindu philosophy, both of which emphasize the importance of doing the right thing. Virtue, or *dharma*, is the guiding principle that underlies all action and refers to the moral and ethical responsibilities that individuals have to themselves and others. In this context, doing the right thing means acting in accordance with one's *dharma*, which involves upholding values such as truth, compassion, and non-violence. Through the practice of *dharma*, individuals can cultivate virtuous qualities such as integrity, selflessness, and humility, which are essential for personal growth and spiritual progress. Ultimately, the pursuit of virtue and the practice of *dharma* are grounded in the belief that living a good and ethical life is not only beneficial for oneself, but also for society as a whole. By doing the right thing and living in accordance with *dharma*, individuals can contribute to the greater good and create a more just and harmonious world.

The role of ethics in fulfilling one's dharma examines the role of ethics in fulfilling one's dharma. It emphasizes the importance of leading a moral and ethical life in fulfilling one's duty and purpose in life, as well as in creating positive *karma*. The right actions performed by one determine the moral part of dharma and the ethical values followed by one determine the virtue part of the dharma.

CHAPTER 10

DHARMA, FORGIVENESS, AND RELATIONSHIPS

*F*orgiveness is a powerful and transformative practice that has the potential to bring healing and growth to our lives, relationships, and communities. In Hindu philosophy, the concept of forgiveness is deeply connected to the principles of *karma* and *dharma*, suggesting that the act of forgiving can help us break free from the cycle of negative actions and consequences, and cultivate a sense of compassion and empathy for ourselves and others. In this chapter, we will explore the power of forgiveness in Hindu philosophy, examining how it is related to the principles of *karma* and *dharma*, and considering the ways in which it can help us let go of resentment, bitterness, and anger. We will also explore the challenges and obstacles that can arise in the practice of forgiveness and offer practical guidance for cultivating forgiveness in our lives.

Forgiveness is a transformative practice that has been celebrated across cultures and religions for its ability to bring about healing, growth, and renewal. In Hindu philosophy, the concept of forgiveness is deeply rooted in the principles of *karma* and *dharma*, suggesting that the act of forgiving can help us break free from the cycle of negative actions and consequences and cultivate a sense of compassion and empathy for ourselves and others.

At the core of the concept of forgiveness in Hindu philosophy is the idea that our actions have consequences and that the negative consequences of our actions can accumulate over time, creating a karmic debt that must be repaid. <u>The act of forgiving can help us release this debt and break free from the cycle of negative actions and consequences.</u> It is a way of acknowledging the inherent value and dignity of all beings and recognizing that our actions have the power to either create suffering or alleviate it.

In addition to its karmic implications, the practice of forgiveness is also closely related to the principles of *dharma*, or right action. Forgiveness is seen as a way of aligning our actions with our highest values and principles and cultivating a sense of equanimity and detachment in the face of life's challenges. It is a way of accepting what is and letting go of the past to move forward with clarity and purpose.

Despite its many benefits, forgiveness can be a challenging and complex practice. It requires a willingness to let go of our grievances and resentments, and a willingness to see the humanity and inherent worth of those who have hurt us. <u>It can also require time, patience, and a deep commitment to our own growth and healing.</u>

To cultivate forgiveness in our lives, it is important to start with ourselves. This means acknowledging our own mistakes and shortcomings and offering ourselves the same compassion and empathy that we would offer to others. It also means recognizing that forgiveness is a process and that it may take time and effort to fully let go of our own pain and hurt.

In addition to cultivating self-forgiveness, it is also important to practice forgiveness toward others. This may involve a willingness to see the humanity and inherent worth of those who have hurt us, and to let go of our desire for revenge or retribution. It may also involve a willingness to set boundaries and communicate our own needs and values, while also extending empathy and compassion to those who have hurt us.

Ultimately, the practice of forgiveness is a powerful tool for cultivating compassion, empathy, and spiritual growth. It is a way of breaking free from the cycle of negative actions and consequences and opening ourselves up to the possibilities of healing, growth, and transformation.

Relationships are a fundamental aspect of human experience, shaping our sense of identity, purpose, and fulfillment. In Hindu philosophy, the principles of *karma* and *dharma* play a central role in shaping our relationships with others, suggesting that our actions and intentions have a profound impact on the quality of our interpersonal connections. In this chapter, we will explore the concept of *karma* in relation to our relationships with others, examining how our actions and intentions shape our interactions with family members, friends, romantic partners, and others. We will also consider the implications of this idea for our understanding of love, compassion, and empathy, and explore how it can help us cultivate deeper and more meaningful relationships with others.

Our relationships with others are shaped by a variety of factors, including our upbringing, social environment, and personal values. However, in Hindu philosophy, the principles of *karma* and *dharma* suggest that our actions and intentions have a significant impact on the quality of our interpersonal connections. *Karma* refers to the law of cause and effect, suggesting that the consequences of our actions and intentions are inevitably reflected to us, shaping our future experiences. *Dharma*, on the other hand, refers to our duty or purpose in life, suggesting that we have a responsibility to act in accordance with our moral principles and spiritual values.

When we apply these principles to our relationships with others, we can see that our actions and intentions towards them have a profound impact on the quality of our connections. For example, if we act with kindness, empathy, and compassion toward others, we are likely to attract similar qualities from them, creating a positive feedback loop that strengthens our relationship. On the other hand, if we act with hostility, dishonesty, or insensitivity, we are likely to encounter similar responses from others, potentially damaging or even destroying our connection.

This idea has important implications for our understanding of love and compassion. If we view love as a feeling that we simply experience towards others, we may overlook the importance of our actions and intentions towards them. However, if we view love as an intentional act of kindness, empathy, and compassion towards others, we can see how our actions shape our experience of love and our connections with others. Similarly, if we view compassion as an intentional act of empathy and understanding toward others, we can see how it can help us cultivate deeper and more meaningful relationships.

In addition to these ideas, *karma,* and *dharma* can also help us cultivate a sense of responsibility for our relationships with others. Rather than viewing our relationships as something that happens to us, we can see them as opportunities to act in accordance with our values and principles. This can help us cultivate a sense of purpose and fulfillment in our connections with others, allowing us to build deeper, more meaningful relationships.

Overall, the principles of *karma* and *dharma* can help us cultivate deeper and more meaningful relationships with others. By recognizing the impact of our actions and intentions, and cultivating a sense of responsibility for our connections with others, we can create a positive feedback loop of kindness, empathy, and compassion that strengthens our relationships and enriches our lives.

Way of Life - Purpose & Moksha

CHAPTER 11

SALVATION AND LIBERATION

*T*he concept of *karma* suggests that our actions have consequences that extend far beyond our immediate circumstances, shaping the course of our lives and the lives of those around us. At the same time, however, we often operate under the illusion of control – that is, the belief that we have the power to shape our destinies through sheer force of will. In this chapter, we will explore the concept of the illusion of control, examining how it can lead us astray in our pursuit of personal and spiritual fulfillment. We will also consider the role that surrendering and acceptance play in Hindu philosophy and explore how they can help us cultivate a sense of equanimity and detachment in the face of life's challenges. Ultimately, we will see how the principles of *karma* and *dharma* can help us navigate the complexities of life, and find a deeper sense of purpose and meaning in our journey.

Salvation and liberation are two concepts that are often used interchangeably, but they have different meanings in different religious and philosophical traditions. In Christianity, salvation generally refers to being saved from sin and its consequences, and attaining eternal life in heaven through faith in Jesus Christ. In contrast, liberation in Hinduism and Buddhism refers to breaking free from the cycle of birth and death and attaining enlightenment or *nirvana*, which is a state of ultimate peace and freedom from suffering.

The concept of the illusion of control is a fascinating topic that explores the tension between our desire for agency and the limits of our power. In this chapter, we will delve into this idea and examine how it can impact our spiritual and personal growth. We will explore how our belief in our ability to control our lives can lead us astray, causing us to ignore the subtle workings of *karma* and the universe. We will also consider how surrender and acceptance can help us cultivate a sense of detachment and equanimity in the face of life's challenges.

The Hindu concept of surrender and acceptance is particularly relevant in this context, as it offers a powerful antidote to the illusion of control. By recognizing our limited ability to control the world around us, we can begin to let go of our attachment to outcomes and focus instead on cultivating a sense of inner peace and contentment. Through this process, we can learn to accept what life brings us with equanimity and grace, recognizing that everything that happens is ultimately for our highest good.

Throughout this chapter, we will also draw upon the principles of *karma* and *dharma*, exploring how they can help us navigate the complexities of life and find deeper meaning and purpose in our journey. By recognizing the interplay between our actions and the larger forces of the universe, we can cultivate a sense of humility and reverence for the mysteries of life, allowing us to surrender to its flow and embrace its unfolding with open hearts and minds.

In Hindu philosophy, the concepts of *karma*, reincarnation, and liberation are inextricably linked, representing a profound and complex understanding of the nature of existence and the ultimate goal of human life. These ideas suggest that our actions in this life will shape our destiny in future lives and that we can achieve liberation from the cycle of birth and rebirth by attaining a state of spiritual enlightenment. In this chapter, we will explore the intricate relationship between these ideas, examining how they inform our understanding of identity, purpose, and meaning. We will also consider the different paths to liberation that are described in Hindu philosophy and explore how these ideas can help us cultivate a sense of compassion, equanimity, and spiritual fulfillment in our lives.

Hindu philosophy has long been associated with the concepts of *karma*, reincarnation, and liberation, which are intricately linked and form the foundation of its worldview. At its core, Hinduism teaches that our actions in this life will shape our destiny in future lives, and that we can break free from the cycle of birth and rebirth by attaining spiritual enlightenment or liberation, also known as *moksha*.

The concept of *karma* refers to the idea that every action we take has consequences that ripple out into the universe and affect us in this life and beyond. The quality of our actions, whether positive or negative, determines our *karma*, and this will affect our future lives and circumstances. This can be seen as a form of cosmic justice that seeks to balance the scales of the universe.

Reincarnation is the belief that the soul is eternal and is reborn into a new body after death. The cycle of birth and rebirth continues until the soul achieves liberation, and this cycle is driven by the concept of *karma*. It is believed that the soul carries the imprints of past actions, which determine the circumstances of its future lives.

The ultimate goal of human life, according to Hinduism, is to achieve liberation or *moksha*. This is a state of spiritual enlightenment that is attained when the soul is freed from the cycle of birth and rebirth. It is believed that achieving *moksha* liberates the soul from the cycle of suffering and allows it to merge with the divine, achieving eternal peace and bliss.

There are various paths to liberation in Hindu philosophy, including *karma yoga, bhakti yoga,* and *jnana yoga. Karma yoga* involves the path of action and service, where one strives to perform their duties without attachment to the fruits of their actions. *Bhakti yoga* involves the path of devotion and love, where one seeks to connect with the divine through prayer, worship, and devotion. *Jnana yoga* involves the path of knowledge and wisdom, where one seeks to attain spiritual enlightenment through self-inquiry and contemplation.

Understanding the concepts of *karma,* reincarnation, and liberation can help us cultivate a deeper sense of compassion, equanimity, and spiritual fulfillment in our lives. It can also help us to take responsibility for our actions and recognize the interconnectedness of all beings. By living a life that is guided by the principles of *karma* and *dharma,* we can strive to create positive *karma* and contribute to the betterment of the world. Ultimately, the pursuit of spiritual liberation offers a profound sense of purpose and meaning, guiding us toward the highest possible expression of ourselves.

The concept of the afterlife varies greatly across different religions. In many belief systems, the afterlife is seen as a continuation of the soul or spirit after physical death, with the nature of the afterlife being shaped by one's actions and beliefs during life. For example, in Hinduism, it is believed that the soul is reborn into another physical body after death, with the quality of that rebirth being determined by one's *karma.* In Buddhism, the ultimate goal is to achieve enlightenment and escape the cycle of rebirth altogether, entering into a state of *nirvana.* In Christianity, the afterlife is often described as either heaven or hell, with the destination being determined by one's faith and adherence to the teachings of Jesus Christ. In Islam, the afterlife is described as a continuation of the soul after death, with the quality of that afterlife being determined by one's adherence to the teachings of the Quran and the Hadith.

Across many religions, the concept of the afterlife serves as a way of providing meaning and purpose to life, as well as offering the possibility of redemption and eternal life beyond physical death. In a way realizing death is inevitable makes one live a purposeful life.

CHAPTER 12

SOME MORE BITE-SIZED THOUGHTS

*T*his chapter lists some of the metaphysics research concepts related to humans and nature and below are some of the key concepts, food for thought.

1. The Scientific Study of Life Values: This field of research aims to understand the subjective experiences, beliefs, and values that shape human behavior and decision-making. Through empirical studies and surveys, researchers seek to identify common values across cultures and explore how they influence individual and societal outcomes.

2. You, Me, and Machines: As technology continues to advance, the relationship between humans and machines becomes increasingly complex. This field of research explores the implications of this relationship for individual identity, social structures, and ethical considerations.

3. Maya and Metaphysics: Maya is a concept in Hindu philosophy that refers to the illusory nature of the material world. This topic delves into the metaphysical

implications of this idea, exploring the nature of reality and the relationship between perception and truth.

4. The Balancing Dance of Nature: This concept refers to the dynamic interplay between different elements of nature, which are constantly shifting and adapting to maintain balance and harmony. It highlights the interconnectedness and interdependence of all things in the natural world.

5. Quantum Physics and Quantum Biology: The principles of quantum physics have increasingly been applied to the study of biological systems, revealing new insights into the fundamental nature of life and consciousness.

6. Ignorance and suffering: This statement is rooted in Hinduism and Buddhism philosophy, suggesting that the root of all suffering is a lack of understanding or awareness. It emphasizes the importance of cultivating wisdom and insight to attain a state of liberation or enlightenment.

7. Intention is what makes an action have good or bad karma: In Hindu philosophy, karma is understood as the law of cause and effect, where our actions and intentions have consequences that shape our future experiences. This idea highlights the importance of cultivating positive intentions to create positive karmic outcomes.

8. Are achievers successful? This research topic explores the distinction between achievement and success, suggesting that they are not necessarily synonymous. It raises questions about the nature of success and the factors that contribute to a fulfilling and meaningful life.

9. Winning & Defeating - As the saying goes, it is easy to defeat someone, but it is difficult to win them. This area of research is about the importance of building positive relationships and communication skills to achieve successful outcomes in interpersonal interactions.

10. Success vs Winning: This topic explores the distinction between success and winning, suggesting that success is more closely aligned with personal fulfillment and meaning while winning is focused on competition and external validation.

11. Journey before destination or Means over the ends: This research area is the importance of the process and the journey, rather than solely focusing on the result. It suggests that how we achieve our goals are just as (or even more) important as the outcomes.

CHAPTER 13

LIVING A LIFE OF PURPOSE

The pursuit of a meaningful and purposeful life is a universal human aspiration and is central to the teachings of many spiritual traditions, including Hindu philosophy. In Hinduism, the concept of *dharma* provides a framework for understanding our individual purpose and role in the world. In this chapter, we will explore the concept of *dharma* and its relationship to living a life of purpose. We will examine the different ways in which *dharma* can manifest in our lives and explore the challenges and opportunities that arise when we seek to align our individual purpose with the larger moral and spiritual universe. We will also consider how living a life of purpose can provide us with a sense of fulfillment, meaning, and connection to something greater than ourselves.

Throughout this book, we have explored the profound and complex ideas that underlie Hindu philosophy, examining how concepts such as *karma*, *dharma*, *moksha*, and rebirth can help us understand the nature of existence and our place in the world. We have seen that these ideas have deep implications for the way we live our lives, suggesting that our actions are intimately connected to our spiritual destiny and that our pursuit of material success and individual freedom is subject to larger moral and spiritual principles.

In this final chapter, we will bring together these different threads of thought, exploring how the principles of *karma* and *dharma* can provide a guiding path for our lives. We will consider the challenges and opportunities that arise from living a life based on these principles and explore how we can cultivate a sense of purpose, meaning, and fulfillment by aligning our actions with the larger moral and spiritual universe.

We will also reflect on how the ideas presented in this book can help us navigate the challenges of modern life and consider the implications of these ideas for our understanding of human nature and the ultimate purpose of existence. By bringing together the insights and perspectives presented throughout this book, we can gain a deeper appreciation of the richness and complexity of various philosophies, and of the profound wisdom that it offers for those seeking a path to spiritual fulfillment and a more meaningful life.

Purposeful life involves discovering our unique talents, strengths, and passions, and using them to contribute to the well-being of others and the larger world. In Hindu philosophy, the concept of *dharma* provides a framework for understanding our individual purpose and role in the world. *Dharma* is often translated as "duty," "righteousness," or "law," but it encompasses much more than that. It is a complex and multifaceted concept that includes our moral and ethical obligations, our social responsibilities, our spiritual aspirations, and our individual talents and interests.

Living a life of purpose also involves a commitment to personal growth and transformation. It requires us to confront our fears, limitations, and self-doubt, and to cultivate qualities such as courage, resilience, and compassion. This process can be challenging and uncomfortable at times, but it is essential for our spiritual and emotional well-being. By embracing our vulnerabilities and weaknesses, we open ourselves up to the possibility of growth and transformation, and we become more authentic and integrated as individuals.

Living a life of purpose is not always easy, and it often involves making difficult choices and sacrifices. It requires us to let go of our attachments and desires, and to prioritize our values and principles above our personal interests. However, when we live in alignment with our *dharma*, we experience a sense of inner peace and contentment that transcends the ups and downs of daily life. We become part of something larger than ourselves, and our actions and intentions have a positive impact on the world around us.

In conclusion, living a life of purpose is an essential aspect of human flourishing, and it is central to the teachings of many spiritual traditions, including Hindu philosophy. By discovering our unique purpose and aligning our actions and intentions with our *dharma*, we can experience a sense of fulfillment, meaning, and connection to something greater than ourselves. We can use our talents and resources to contribute to the well-being of others and the larger world, and we can cultivate qualities such as courage, resilience, and compassion that help us navigate the challenges of life with grace and wisdom.

CONCLUSION

The ideas and concepts explored in this list center around the nature of reality, *karma*, *dharma*, and spirituality. *Karma* and *dharma* are seen as powerful forces that influence the course of our lives, with *karma* representing the law of cause and effect and *dharma* representing our duty or purpose. Inaction and detachment from material desires are seen as ways to achieve spiritual growth and liberation.

Luck and the Matthew Effect are discussed, as well as the importance of balance and moderation in all things. The illusion of control is explored, and the idea that we suffer more in imagination than in reality is emphasized.

The concepts of reincarnation and forgiveness are explored, along with the importance of wise relationships and social justice. The environment and living a life of purpose are also touched upon.

Faith and spirituality are seen as important components of a meaningful life, and the idea that ignorance is the cause of all suffering is discussed. The importance of intention and journey over destination is emphasized.

Overall, these concepts point toward a way of living that is focused on personal growth, spirituality, and fulfilling one's purpose while maintaining balance and detachment from material desires.

In conclusion, it is practically experienced by all that action or inaction is the cause of the positive or negative outcomes and so executing the freewill is vital to move forward with life, one of the convincing answers related to freewill actioning is that we are seeing opportunities because of past *karma* and now our present decisive action based on our freewill choice in a dharmic way sets us up for the future destiny.

*Hope this book gave you more insights into some
of the important life aspects and you learned some
things that you can imbibe too. One may also say that
you were able to understand the way of life with this
book due to your good karma, do you agree?*

**MAY THE ALMIGHTY BLESS YOU TO DO RIGHT
KARMA FOLLOWING THE *DHARMA***

ABOUT THE AUTHOR

Dr. Sunil Kumar Kodichath is a researcher and mentor for various Ph.D. research enthusiasts in the field of management and human resources. He is also a guest speaker at various institutions across India.

This book is based on questions raised by myself and other like-minded people on the subject of metaphysics and on practical experience gained during the 20 years of handling people as a human resource professional.

Dr. Sunil is based out of India and for any appreciation or point of view or comments please reach out to sk.sunilkma4@gmail.com.

www.ingramcontent.com/pod-product-compliance
Lightning Source LLC
Chambersburg PA
CBHW051234160726
47994CB00002B/882